Planning
Children's
Birthday
Parties

Libby and Penny's
Survival Guide

Libby Worsley Crouch
Penny Barlow Liston

DEDICATION

To our fantastic children and grandchildren
and to the many students we have so enjoyed.
With love, Libby and Penny

AKA Grandma BB and Amma Gramma/Ammie

ACKNOWLEDGMENTS

We would like to thank our many friends for their encouragement and feedback. A special thanks to Patti Phillips, Kate Rakoci, Lisa Schleier, Sharon Doyle Ward, Christie Crouch, Michael Pisani, and Paul Beiley for their editorial suggestions. A huge thank you to the creative genius of our illustrator Chellie Buzzeo.

Getting Started

Party planning begins the moment you decide to have a party. Whether you purchase commercial party materials or create your own, you will need to know what to do with the children from the moment they arrive until they go home. Libby and Penny focus on the details of the party and the implementation of a plan that will create a memorable day for your child.

This book is a guide to the nitty-gritty that will be the soul of the party no matter what theme has been chosen. If a party is kept simple, if the child is included in the planning, if the guest list is limited, and if there is an organized party

> The planning can be as much fun as the event.

plan, you will have a great party. The planning can be as much fun as the event; be sure to include your child in the early stages so they can enjoy the anticipation and begin to develop organizational skills. We are including numerous suggestions with explanations as to why they are important and assist parents in the experience of giving a child's birthday party. Our personal and teaching experiences have provided us with both a practical and academic understanding necessary for creating such a book.

As teachers we have many years of experience working with children. Later, as parents, we recognized our years of teaching provided us with valuable expertise. The need for creating timelines, schedules, an organized plan, age appropriate activities, preparing children, and reviewing manners and behaviors are essential when working with children and planning a birthday party.

As beginning teachers we experienced, firsthand, the chaos of an unplanned, unorganized party. How to give a class party was not covered in our education. We were members of a team of new teachers working together, and it was our first party of the school year. The parent committee assured us the party was planned, but being rookie teachers, we didn't ask for the plan. The parents arrived with games, crafts, and snacks. The students didn't know what was expected of them, we were not sure of the plan, and none of us were prepared for what developed. As the party progressed the children's behavior rapidly deteriorated into boundless chaotic energy. Pandemonium was taking place right in front of us. Recess started early that day!

This early teaching experience made a very strong impression upon us. We made a point of being very organized for future parties.

What separates Libby and Penny's survival guide from other resources is the attention given to details such as: the importance of a well-planned party timeline based on the activity levels and the ages of children, the reasons behind the suggestions, the importance of social skills, age appropriate activities, understanding budget, communication between parent and child, preparing a child for the unexpected, gift giving and receiving, safety, preparing the party area, and family traditions. Purchasing materials, deciding on activities and crafts, decorations, and obtaining cake ideas are all important. However, without a plan and schedule there is an opportunity for chaos.

As we began to write this book, we had many giggles over the memory of that first classroom party and we realized that is the reason we knew we could help parents plan a successful children's birthday party. We truly want your party to create happy lasting memories and a most positive experience for all.

Our survival guide contains five sections and can be read cover to cover for the full experience or browsed using the table of contents to obtain what is required for your immediate needs:

- Chapters 1 – 2 give an overview including first, toddler, and preschool parties.

- Chapter 3 provides descriptive plans from weeks before the party to days after, a specific schedule for party day, and a template for creating a party plan.

- Chapters 4 – 9 offer budget, guest list, invitations, manners, gift giving, safety, behaviors,traditions and party timeline.

- Chapters 10 – 19 offer a planning template and detailed theme parties.

- Chapters 20 – 22 list art/craft activities, game ideas and supplies/shopping list.

Shouldn't we know how to give a child's birthday party, we remember going to them? Adult memories of childhood events are recalled via a child's level of awareness. As children we didn't concern ourselves with what adults were doing to keep the party going. Now, as parents we realize how much goes into creating a party.

The First, Toddler and Preschool Parties

You have survived one or more years of parenting. Are you prepared for the next challenge? The thought of planning and putting on a child's birthday party can challenge the best of us.

The birthday party is a great format for teaching your child social skills which assist in making and keeping friends. When children begin to know and use the social rules and guidelines of their culture they feel accepted as members of a group. Knowing how to communicate with others increases confidence and self-esteem.

The child being honored at the party is the center of attention; they are dealing with the experience of being important, special, and they might feel unsure as to why. Using *Libby and Penny's Survival Guide* will alleviate some of those concerns. The let down after a wild, over-the-top, unorganized party can be avoided. When involved in the process, a child knows what is expected and there is less misunderstanding the day of the party.

Throughout the book many ideas are suggested, the intent is to select only a few to do at any one party. There are many ways to allow your child to participate. Pick and choose ideas according to your child's age and abilities, build on these as your child gets older and becomes ready for more planning responsibilities.

One of the important first decisions is whether the party is going to be a family gathering in celebration of the child's birth or a child-centered party.

*A **first birthday party*** is often a celebration for the parents to enjoy with aunts, uncles, grandparents, cousins, and friends. Traditionally this party is like many family gatherings with the addition of birthday cake and gifts. This tradition may continue until the child is able to attend parties on their own. That will usually take place when children are in school or about the age of 5.

There is a comfort in knowing the children are surrounded by family and close friends. New parents are happy to be celebrating their first year of parenthood. Having a plan,

 some child centered activities, and areas set aside for children to play will make the party easier for parents.

For the safety of all the children attending, it is best to have a designated area or areas for youngsters to play. These can be identified by placing a tablecloth or blanket on the floor to create the boundaries for each activity. Place toys according to age or interest in the designated areas; blocks, dolls, trucks, etc. An additional option is to cover a work/play table so children and adults may sit together. Set out puzzles, stickers, crayons, play dough and paper. Avoid scissors, paints and activities that need extra supervision at this very young age.

Parents of a 1-year-old will often not have toys for older children available, so ask the parents of those guests to bring something for their older child to play with. With preparation every child will have something to do.

The birthday party will evolve and change as the child matures. The celebration will shift from a party planned by adults for adults and children, to a party that is planned by the parent but with the child contributing ideas. Over time the event will become a child-centered party, with the adult and birthday child making the decisions.

All girl and all boy parties become popular as interests change. Girls enjoy interacting, communicating, and closely working together doing small motor activities while boys often enjoy using their entire bodies doing activities that extend over large areas of space. Birthday parties change according to the basic stages and development of children.

A detailed outline for a family gathering birthday party can be found with the theme parties. The first birthday party is considered a family gathering in this book.

Birthday party for preschool children

Parents of preschool children often want to attend the parties of their young children, not only to be sure their child is comfortable but to enjoy the camaraderie and friendship of the other parents. Often the guest list will include the parents and siblings of the invited child. This creates additional mouths to feed, additional materials for the siblings, activities suitable for a wider age range, and the need for more physical space and more planning by the party giver. Preparation is essential for this kind of party.

> A birthday party is not the same as a family gathering. A child's birthday party is focused around and is for children. A family gathering is unstructured, unlike a birthday party which has a more structured approach.

This is no longer a family gathering. Serving alcohol to parents during a child's birthday party is inappropriate. A parent who has had too much could affect the safety of the children at the party and while traveling home.

When parents are to attend, ask them to assist in a specific way, such as overseeing an activity table, helping with food preparation, setting up an activity, or monitoring the children. Encouraging parents in attendance to help will make the party a positive experience for all ages. Ask parents to confirm whether they will be attending when they reply to the invitation. Get a count of how many children from each family will be coming and their ages. Be sure a parent is planning to stay if they bring siblings of the invited guest.

Young children often do not interact with one another while playing as much as they tend to play alongside each other (parallel play), frequently doing similar activities. They are often not yet ready for sharing and interacting with one another.

A child's birthday party is not the same as a family gathering. A child's birthday party is focused around and is for children. A family gathering is unstructured, unlike a birthday party which has a more structured approach. Some parents may not be accustomed to the idea of a supervised and organized party. Nonetheless it can be fun for both the adults and their children.

Play areas

To have a safe and fun party with multiple ages attending, organization is key. This birthday party is based on parent-child interaction. Create play areas so the children and parents can move from place to place for different activities. A child's attention span can be from 5 minutes to 15 minutes according to the amount of interest and adult interaction they are getting.

> A child's attention span can be from 5 minutes to 15 minutes according to the amount of interest and adult interaction they are getting.

Think of the activities your child enjoys and create play areas using those activities. The children will enjoy going from area to area with their parents.

Make a list of activities available and where they will be set up so everyone will know what they can do during the party. Make a schedule for all to see or print one for each adult.

It may be difficult to provide enough physical space for the children and their parents at a dinner table. If that is the case, have the party table set for the children and encourage the parents to assist and watch the children. Everyone can join in for singing and blowing out the birthday candles. Have enough cake for all.

Opening of gifts can be a shared event for gift-giver and receiver. Set the gifts in a circle on the floor and have the children sit by the gifts they brought. Have them take turns giving their gifts to the birthday child. The children can share the opening experience. This could be the moment your child hands out goodie bags.

> Time spent together is a lasting gift.

This is a great time to take a photo of each child with the birthday child. The photo can be sent along with or as a thank-you note. By taking the time to organize a party in this way you have created the gift of a shared memory.

Blueprint for Planning School-Aged Parties:

Before, During, and After

This chapter is an abbreviated version of the party plan.
Specific details are discussed in future chapters.

Making the plan

- *Select a theme:* Consider ideas from both the child and parents. Think of all the items you already have that will work for your theme. Then make a list of additional items needed to be purchased.

- *Create the Budget:* Consider possible costs— invitations, envelopes, stamps, foods, decorations, cups, plates, table covering, streamers, flatware, party favors, extra scissors, paint, crayons, project materials, and goodie bags.

- *List the possible guests:* Remember the rule of thumb that the number of children attending matches the child's age on their birthday.

- *Select date and time:* Be specific.

- *Select games and activities that keep everyone participating:* Keep the children engaged and involved in the party. An organized age-based party will be orderly and easy to keep under control. Balance the games between high and low activity. Too many high-activity games can over-stimulate and wear out the guests, just as too many quiet activities can bring on fidgety behavior. You know how long your child's attention span is, base the timing on what you know. Older children can concentrate on an activity longer without losing interest.

> When inviting just the boys (or girls) from class either invite everyone or limit the number so not to omit just one child.

Select games and activities that keep everyone participating. Games of elimination remove children from involvement, at which time they can become bored and wander away from adult supervision. It is not as much fun sitting on the sidelines while the other kids play in the game.

> If you are planning a craft or art activity, do it before mealtime so the creations can dry before being taken home.

- *Be flexible:* Something could go wrong, and if you have done your planning you will be ready for a quick change. Remember, the children do not know what was to happen; they will only experience what does happen.

Practice games and activities

What art and craft project does your child like? Their friends will most likely enjoy similar things. This is a great way to start choosing activities. Practice explaining the rules and have your child perform each game or activity in advance. This is a win-win situation for parent and child. You will know how long each activity will take by observing your child doing it. Write down how long it took from the moment you gave the directions to the end; the time spent might surprise you. Your child will also gain confidence in carrying out the activity and later feel good about being able to help others. You can change the name of activities to fit your theme. Hot potato can become space ship pass or pass the dinosaur. Duck, Duck, Goose can become Superman, Superman, Spiderman for a Superhero party.

One month in advance

- Create invitations.

- Fill out guest list form.

- Have guest list form in an easy-to-find place to record RSVPs.

- Decide what items will be needed for party.

- If you are having a theme party based on a book, TV show, movie or special topic, start to collect things like stickers, toys, books, and DVD's on the subject to share at the party. Showing a 10-15 minute DVD can set the theme. If a favorite book is the theme, plan to read it or a favorite part. If paperback books are available on the selected theme, they could be a great party favor or game prizes.

- Send out invitations at least two weeks ahead of time.

Two weeks before party

- Practice all games and projects. If you purchase a special project be sure to have your child practice and time the process. The extra expense of one additional craft project is worth the cost. It may be too difficult, additional items are needed, the allotted time is wrong, or it wasn't what was expected. The extra one made in advance can be a sample.

- Purchase the items you need and put them in a special area. Anticipation is part of the fun, watching the area, shelf or box fill up, builds excitement and teaches your child organization. Purchase party table wear if not using your own tablecloths, plates, cups, etc.

The week of the party

- Contact people who have not responded.

- Be sure all items you need are in one place to avoid later surprises.

- Buy or prepare cake.

- Be sure your camera is charged and ready.

- If you are decorating the house, do it in advance so you can enjoy the fruits of your labor and take photos.

- Ask and confirm that an adult friend or teenager will assist the day of the party.

- Discuss expectations with your child, such as greeting guests, gift giving, thank-you notes, etc.

- Encourage your child to store special personal items where they won't be seen.

- Set aside containers with all necessary items. Organize the items in baskets or boxes. Include list of materials needed along with directions for each activity. Label the outside of each box so if they are stacked, you can still see what's inside. Creating this organized plan allows a parent or other helper to easily find the items needed for each game or activity.

- Purchase or collect items for activities and decorations. Have enough tools for each child. For instance, two pairs of scissors for five children may cause supply and demand difficulties and slow down the process.

- Keep a checklist of who has replied. Make note of food allergies and ask for contact information if a parent may need to be reached during the party.

- Create the party timeline. (Use example in chapter 9)

- Purchase and prepare food.

- Prepare area for the party. Decorations can be kept at a minimum. Something eye-catching that attracts the guest's attention upon arriving will set the theme.

- Keep in mind possible hazards: electrical cords, lamps or breakables at children's level, etc.

- Enjoy the process of decorating the room and table. Encourage your child to assist.

- Look over safety tips.

- Make a list of the activities, and party time line for the parent or adult assistant to refer to during party.

- Have everything prepared in advance. Get a good night's sleep so you and the birthday child will be rested and ready.

Before party time

- Put out balloons or a Birthday banner to identify party house.

- Have RSVP list by door to quickly check off children as they arrive and add parents' cell phone numbers.

- Have food ready to serve.

Party time

- Birthday child and parent should welcome guests at the door.

- Guests will take part in a welcoming activity until everyone arrives. Think of something fun for the guests to do while waiting for all to arrive. You could have supplies out for decorating a goodie bag. Each person will have their own bag to decorate and write their name on. This can be as simple as a brown bag or as elaborate as fabric sacks. Any open-ended activity will work at this time such as beading, making nametags, blocks, dolls, coloring, or clay.

- Introduce yourself (and your spouse and adult assistants) to the children; establish how you want the children to identify you. This is important because you are the authority for the next two hours. "I am Mrs. Liston, Miss Ellie, I am Gregory's mom."

- Tell the children what is planned. "We are going to have a great time. We are going to…" You may have a chart showing the plan or simply tell the children, we will play some games, do this and that activity, have a snack, open gifts, play a game, etc. Show a short DVD, read a story or book, hand out costumes, tell the guests what they are going to be doing.

- Children are familiar with teachers giving them objectives. They will feel comfortable knowing what is planned. An objective tells the children the who, what, where, and when of what they will be doing and what is expected of them.

- Explain each game and activity. Give the rules just before each game is played. Explain that they may have played the game before with different rules, but today we are doing it this way. Tell the children you want to be sure they understood. Ask a child to help by repeating the directions to the group. The children hear the directions twice and they participate in the creation of ground rules.

- Select games and activities that keep everyone participating. Games of elimination remove children from involvement. Limit these games with young children.

- If you are planning a craft or art activity, doing it early in the party allows the projects to dry before taking them home.

Activities according to age and stage

We have not indicated the specific ages for many of the party activities. Children develop at different rates and parents are the best judge of their child's abilities. Activities suggested in the book are to be tested by the parent with their child to decide if appropriate.

Fine motor skills develop when the child's muscles in their fingers and hands coordinate with what they see. Children's abilities move from smashing peas with a fork to balancing and lifting peas on a fork. Activities for 2-4 year olds include beading using items with large holes, puzzles with large pieces, and large muscle movement. The 5-6 year olds begin to develop skills like tying their shoes, cutting around shapes and using a knife.

- If items are in front of the children, they will touch them and possibly start before the directions are completed. You could cover the items for the project with a cloth. Show the sample project, give the directions, and begin.

- Hand washing and bathroom breaks before snacks.

- Sit at a table or designated area for eating.

- Opening gifts (chapter 5).

- Game or activity. Wide range of possibilities included in this book.

- Finish up any projects.

- Quiet time, party favors, goodie bags, before preparing to go home.

- **_End of party._** The birthday child thanks each child for attending. It is always a good idea to have a calm organized activity when the parents come for their child.

Days after the party

- Write and send thank-you notes

- Make a memory book of party

4

The Essentials for Surviving

Elementary school age parties

Parties for elementary children are made up of the child's peer group. Often children are dropped off and parents are not expected to stay. We encourage home parties, in the family room, basement, kitchen, back yard, a common room in an apartment, or the neighborhood park. Clearing out the garage, cleaning and adding a coat of paint creates a surprisingly large activity area. Sometimes it is convenient to have the party at a structured party place, such as a pizza

> Determine what your child is expecting to prevent misunderstandings later.

restaurant, amusement facility, party facility, or other child-centered environment. Planning is important for all parties wherever located.

Communication is essential at all ages. Discuss with your child if they want a party this year. It's a crazy idea, yet a good conversation to have with your child. Remind your child of a party you both attended and talk about what they liked or didn't like about it. Some children would prefer just close family members, neighbors, or buddies. Alternating between family and friend parties is a possibility.

Determine what your child is expecting to prevent misunderstandings later. This is the time to discuss limits due to time, space, and costs. One way to set limits might be to count the number of chairs that fit around your table, reminding the child how many people can be invited.

Let The Planning Begin!

Budget

Teaching your child about finances is an important goal for any parent. Children can gain a greater understanding of boundaries and limits when helping to plan the budget. Take into account your child's age and understanding of money and try to include them as much as possible in the budgeting process. Children can understand a budget when it is explained clearly. Using a dollar amount or selecting a few options among a number of possibilities will assist the child in being a part of the decision-making process.

Young children can understand 'either/or' statements such as: shall we have a special project or party favors, either takeout food or homemade, lots of new decorations or use some we already have, spend on this item or that item? These simple decisions are part of the process. When a child knows how much can be spent, along with the expectations of what the money can be used for, they will begin to recognize the most efficient ways to use the funds.

A budget can be related to their everyday lives. A child can understand budget choices when it is related to the money available to them. An example: When a child goes shopping using their own money, they make choices based on what they have in their wallet. That is working within a budget! Remind your child that making a budget for the party is similar to making decisions on spending their own money.

The conversations on budgeting are groundwork for the real-life situations they will face in the future.

> When a child goes shopping using their own money, they make choices based on what they have in their wallet. This teaches working with a budget!

If this is your child's first experience in party budgeting, you will want a guide to costs. Choosing what to purchase can be a lesson in searching the Internet for the products and comparing prices. Items to be considered:

- Invitations
- Envelopes
- Stamps
- Foods
- Decorations
- Cups
- Plates
- Table covering
- Streamers
- Flatware
- Party favors
- Extra scissors
- Paint, crayons
- Project materials
- Goodie bags

Party theme

Decide on a theme with your child or offer a few choices you are willing to do and your child will enjoy. The theme of the party could be something your child already enjoys doing. If your child is wild

> A Traditional Birthday Party as a theme is a good solid standby.

about trucks, cars, animals, firemen, dolls, magic, etc., the theme can be expanded. Other ideas could be art, machines, rocks, dinosaurs, movies, or your child's love of a specific sport or activity. A Traditional Birthday Party as a theme is a good solid standby. With a theme selected, develop the invitations, food, and activities around it.

> We have suggested changing some of the rules of elimination games and renaming games to fit party themes. Discuss these changes with the attending adults so they understand you have not forgotten how to play the game, rather you have consciously made these modifications.

If a theme party is to be based on a book, TV show, or movie, start collecting items such as stickers, toys, books or a DVD on the subject to share at the party. If your theme is emergency vehicles, showing a 15-minute video on them would set the tone when the children arrive. If a book is the theme, plan to read a favorite part or the entire book. If paperback books are available on the theme, they could be a great party favor or game prize.

Use themes that are suitable and timely for children according to their age and abilities. The party should take into account the interests of both the birthday child and guests. Using a theme unique to your family's interests may or may not be of interest to the guests. If guests are not acquainted with a subject, be prepared to make it an educational event. An example would be a bird-watching party, which can then become a learning experience for the guests.

We are encouraging parents to guide their child into the role of being a participant in the planning process. The idea is they will be able to do more each year. But parties which are costly or advanced for an age level could lead to sticky situations. The child may well begin to expect more and more each year. We are not suggesting little girls wouldn't enjoy a manicure, pedicure, and massage when they are 6 years old, but we suggest allowing for those big ticket items to come when they might be more appreciated. Having the first "boy-girl" party, makeup party or spa party can overly expose and sensationalize children to teenage and adult subject matter. Similar concerns arise with regard to parties exploring topics not yet experienced, such as paint guns, fly fishing, or rock climbing. Although your child might excel in a certain activity, the invited children may not have the acquired skills or background. Plan activities the majority of attendees can be successful at.

Guests: Keeping the perfect balance!

The rule of thumb: Invite the number of children equal to the age of the child on that birthday.

> Invite the number of children equal to the age of the child on that birthday.

Therefore, invite five guests if your child is turning 5. This is a manageable number. Manageable means that all the children will likely enjoy themselves throughout the party. Talk with your child about whom they would like to invite and make the list together. This is a good time to find out why they do or do not want someone included. It's also a way to avoid possible concerns or problems.

You may discover a child you intended to invite tends to break toys, isn't polite, or is upsetting to your child. This is the moment to discuss how to handle these life situations. Another circumstance involves children of your personal friends. If the children have participated in play dates and know each other, include them. If they

> One adult with multiple playful children will not be enough. Someone should always be with the children for the sole purpose of keeping all of them safe and engaged in the activities.

have not played together, don't expect them to establish a friendship during a party full of your child's good friends. The situation may make you or your child uncomfortable.

Siblings of the birthday child may be included and may be given some responsibility so they feel an important part of the happenings. Siblings may wish to take part in the preparation or planning, but may not want to be around for the party. Respect their wishes and find a workable compromise. Siblings could be allowed to invite a friend or go to a friend's home while the party is going on. At times, siblings may want to be included in one aspect of the party such as eating the cake or an activity. Whatever works for your family will help maintain a positive experience for the birthday child.

A child wants to feel special and having their parent participating is important to them. If both parents cannot attend, ask a close friend, relative, or babysitter if they would be willing to assist. In case of an emergency, it is always best to have another adult to help. One adult with multiple playful children will not be enough. Someone should always be with the children for the sole purpose of keeping all of them safe and engaged in the activities.

Invitations: They are so much fun to receive!

To snail mail or email. Yes, email is efficient, yet children enjoy getting postal mail. You decide what is best. Some schools provide directories or class contact lists. If email is the only means to obtain an address, email the parent, introduce yourself, explain you are inviting their child to a birthday party, and ask for their address. Do not send the invitations to school with your child to distribute. This could cause hurt feelings for the

> Explain to your child the importance of being thoughtful. Discussing their party plans on the playground or at school will upset uninvited guests.

uninvited. When in doubt, ask the teacher what the rules are for distributing invitations. No matter how discreetly this is done, the other children and observant parents will know who has been left out. Many schools discourage handing out invitations at school.

Create or purchase invitations: Have your child help make some simple decisions such as selecting an invitation. Allow a young child to choose between designs you are willing to use. As children mature, they will be willing to add their own ideas. Purchasing the invitations can be done through a local store or online.

If you choose to create your own invitation, gather your supplies and have the fun of creating a one-of-a-kind invitation. This could be done with the help of the birthday child or as a family project. Postcards are another option and are less expensive to mail.

Address the envelope to the young person who is being invited. When sending in the mail, leave enough time for the guest to receive it and then respond.

Invitation information

- *Theme:* such as Tea Party, Pirate Party, Artist Party, etc.

- *Name of child:* you may want to add nickname if that is what guests will know.

- *Where:* Be specific, and you may want to include a small map.

- *Time:* Be clear on the beginning and end time. Limit the party to 1 ½ to 2 ½ hours. Consider naps and best time of day for both your child and guests.
The day of the party is exciting for your child, so keep in mind how their behavior will change the longer they

When the party is taking place in a public location give the children an identifying item to wear so they can be easily spotted in a crowd. A bandana, hat, T-Shirt, arm band, scarf, etc.

have to wait. Having the party in the morning means less anxious waiting and allows kids to go home after the party to rest or continue their day.

We recommend a party for preschool children to be no more than two hours long; for kindergarten through second grade children, extend it to 2 ½ hours. If you are traveling to a party place with older children, the time will depend on the activities planned. Shorter time favors better control of the children, always a consideration. Children can get wound up and rambunctious when not involved in structured activities.

- *Date:* Friday, May 3. Choose a date for the party far enough in advance to avoid conflicts. Other children may share the same birthday as your child. If possible, check with the other parents to discover if and when they may be planning a party. A date change may be necessary to allow the birthday children and guests to attend both parties. A birthday party, unlike a New Year's Eve party, does not have to take place on a specific date.

- Include in the invitation information on any extras that may be needed: costumes, special clothes, any additional items they should bring.

- *RSVP:* Reply by date (be specific), and include your contact information, which consists of home phone, cell number, and email address. When the parent responds, ask about food allergies, special needs, contact information, and who will be picking up the child.

When guests reply

When parents accept, inform them of the limited guest list so they understand their child's acceptance and attendance is very important to the birthday child and to the success of the party. If a parent asks if they can drop off another sibling, explain the party is for children of the same age group and you will not be prepared or have items for additional children.

Replying to an invitation is a good social skill for children to learn. Children learn by watching, so make a point of letting your child know when RSVP's have been made as well as when you respond to an invitation. A young child can help check off or add a sticker next to the name of a child who is coming to their party. Using the checklist, create the party guest list and keep it near the phone or computer. An older child can check off each guest's name as they respond. This is a great way to keep the birthday child aware of who will be coming.

> When parents accept, inform them of the limited guest list so they understand their child's acceptance and attendance is very important to the birthday child and to the success of the party.

Parents of young children will be the ones who respond to an invitation. This is also a good time to ask the parent for their contact information, and also if their child has any food allergies. Add this information to the guest list. When children are old enough to make a phone call, the invited guest may reply. This gives the invited child the opportunity to respond and is a way to practice good manners on the telephone.

Keeping a list will help in your planning. It will also be used at the party to make sure you have the correct information and then again for the thank-you note list.

Child's Name	Address	Phone	Yes/no	Who's picking up	Special needs	Gift
Alex	123 Brody Ave City, ZIP	555.9876	yes	Mom Caroline	nut allergy	
Gregory	23 Bella St City, ZIP	555.1243	yes	Dad Vincent		
Tatum	432 Enzo St City, ZIP	555.2157	yes	Dad Elliott		
Campbell	8 Francesca St City, ZIP	555.0724	yes	Dad Mike		

The experience of not being invited to a party

There may be a time when your child discovers they were not invited to a party. This is an opportunity to discuss how your child is feeling. Express your understanding, a short open-ended comment: tough, isn't it? Let them know you are familiar with how it feels to miss out: I felt hurt when I wasn't included. Sometimes a child is simply letting you know a fact, checking in with you for your response, and not necessarily looking for an explanation as to why they were not invited.

You can help them problem-solve the reasons why they were not included: location, cost, level of friendship, etc. Ask your child if this person would be on their list of good friends. A party is usually made up of friends who play together and have common interests. This uncomfortable situation could lead to a discussion on how to be a friend and how to develop friendships. This is all part of the process of growing up. Your understanding and guidance will help your child feel comfortable discussing problems and trying to solve them.

Important details!

This is the time to keep your budget in mind. Think of everything that will be needed for food, invitations, stamps, games, activities, decorations, and party favors. Creating a thorough shopping list will help avoid those unnecessary trips to the store at the last minute.

- *Decorations:* The children will be enthusiastically anticipating being at a birthday party. Many of the children will be unfamiliar with your home so everything will be new and different. Decorations are an added bonus; a few well-placed decorations will enrich the theme without creating too much work or expense for the parent. If you have selected a theme from something your child already enjoys, you may have the props (regalia) already available, such as posters, trucks, books, craft supplies, etc. Tie a few balloons outdoors to identify the party location. Decorating the area most used will limit expenses. Decorations can be as simple as colorful paper chains, streamers, ribbons, balloons, and a poster declaring the birthday child's name.

> Make use of materials you have on hand, that's a great way to recycle.

- *Party favors:* Party favors can be an accumulation of the activities and items used during the party. The items used during the party can go home as reminders of the fun they had. Goodie bags and other kinds of favors can be costly extras. The bags can be as simple as a white or brown lunch bag that the children decorate at the party or they can be purchased. Watch for seasonal items on sale. Many basic items can be purchased in advance such as balloons, paper goods, seasonal toys, stickers, etc.

- *Organize materials:* Organize items according to each activity, using containers such as individual boxes or plastic tubs. Purchase or collect items necessary for all the activities and games, including tape, scissors, paper, materials for games, marking pens, etc. Have enough tools for each child, place all the supplies including the directions for each activity into a container. Mark the containers on the outside with the name of the activity and list all items in each container. This will allow for easy visibility if stacking the containers.

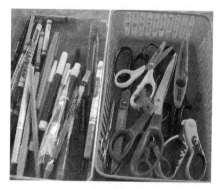

Using this organized method allows for anyone to easily select the container needed for each game or activity.

Anticipation is part of the fun. Watching the area, shelf or box fill up with party items builds excitement and teaches organization.

- *Activities and games:* An organized age-based party will be orderly and easy to keep under control. Balance the games between high and low activity. Allow 10 to 15 minutes per game within a 30 – 45 minute time slot. You know your child's attention span; base the timing on what you know. Older children can concentrate longer on one game or activity.

If the children are enthusiastically enjoying an activity there is no need to switch to the next activity. Allow the children to enjoy the experience. There is no need to stop the fun.

Many games and activities are mentioned both in the themed parties and listed in a later chapter of this book.

- ***Food:*** Select foods that are healthy, appealing, easy to prepare and serve. Time fixing food separates you from overseeing the children. This places an added burden on the other adult supervising. When a parent RSVP's, inquire whether their child has any food allergies. Include your child in food choices. You will also need to decide if you are going to have the children prepare their own party food or if it will be premade for them. This depends on their abilities and if you have allowed time for food-making.

Remember to have children wash their hands with soapy water before and after cooking. Preparing their own snack could be as simple as pouring their own drinks to making a cheese muffin pizza (English muffins with cheese melted on top).

Keep in mind healthy food is easy to serve and enjoyed by children. Veggies with dips, whole wheat breads with protein, and string cheese are often a big hit. Children often enjoy making their own foods and will tend to eat what they have made. Yes, it will be messy and take extra time, but because they participated in the process, they will remember what fun they had.

Consider preparing most of the food in advance and have a simple set-up. The children can help make the food during the party as part of an activity. Be aware of children near a hot barbecue or stove. It is always important to have one or two adults watching the children while an adult is getting the food ready to serve.

Creating place cards with each child's name allows you to arrange the seating. Using place cards can assist in food placement if anyone has a food allergy. Place children next to people they will enjoy sitting with. Or allow the children to select their own places.

> Keep it simple so everyone can enjoy the party.

Singing "Happy Birthday" and enjoying the birthday cake is always an enjoyable part of the celebration. The cake can be the child's favorite flavor decorated with the theme of the party.

Another option is to serve cupcakes clustered together on a cake plate with candles. Or try cake pops, which are smaller cake balls on a stick, for a smaller taste of dessert.

Any way you choose to do a dessert is perfect. This is the time when your own family traditions can be expressed. Be careful with candles as this can become a safety issue.

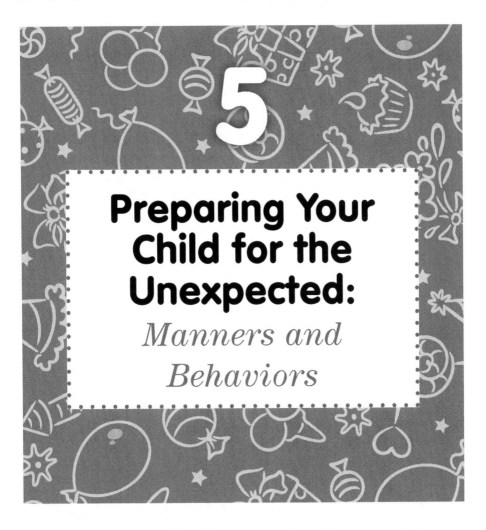

5

Preparing Your Child for the Unexpected:

Manners and Behaviors

We feel that one of the best preparations for your party is to get your child ready for being the center of attention.

That can be both a pleasure and a responsibility. It is always a good idea to prepare your child for what you will be expecting of them. Talk with your child about what will occur at the party. If you begin to prepare them as you are getting the invitations ready and remind them later of what will happen during their party, they will be ready.

"Best behavior" is just a phrase to a child and needs to be explained. For a birthday party it includes greeting guests, introducing the guests to each other, remembering to say please and thank you, and taking time to be with each guest.

Manners and behaviors taught at a young age will last a lifetime. A child may not fully know what the adult expectations might be. For a birthday party it includes greeting guests, introducing the guests to each other, remembering to say "please" and "thank you," and taking time to be with each guest. These expectations are skills children can learn. You will want your child to be a gracious and polite host, so be sure to talk about these manners beforehand.

You are the role model, and your child will mimic your behavior. Then, when it is their turn, proper behavior will be a natural response. We know this is true because we have seen children repeating a phrase or an action identical to what their parent did.

The element of surprise, while enjoyable for the giver, is not necessarily as grand for the receiver. Surprise is by definition a shock. For many children there is no need for additional elements that could overwhelm them. Be aware of your child's comfort level; surprises could distress and confuse them. The surprise arrival of a costumed character may frighten toddlers, while it might be a welcome addition for elementary-aged children.

Some events cannot be controlled, such as the weather, the friend who can't come, or the child who becomes ill. Let your child know that there are possible things that may happen or may not. Avoid setting your child up for disappointment.

Greeting guests

Being at the door with the birthday child gives you the opportunity to meet the parents and confirm their cell phone numbers.

Have your child with you at the door. Encourage them to say hello and welcome guests to the party. Have your child shake hands and tell them they are glad they are here. The child may need to introduce the guest to you. An example would be, "Mom, this is my friend Philip. We are in the same classroom at school. Philip, this is my mom, Mrs. Crouch." Then mom says, "It is so nice to meet you, Philip." The guest may respond and introduce their parent to you, if not introduce yourself to the parent. Modeling behavior for your child will build confidence and provide comfort in knowing they are making their guests welcome, which in turn makes the guests feel comfortable. These techniques can be introduced when you feel your child is ready.

Remember our rule of thumb, that the number of guests invited should be no more than the age of the birthday child, so the greeting process should not take long. We recommend a parent be at the door with the birthday child; this gives both of you the opportunity to meet the children's parents and for you to confirm their cell phone numbers. It is always a good thing to be prepared for an emergency.

Gift giving

We have noticed opening gifts is not always done at the party. Guests spend time and energy buying or creating gifts and hope they will be appreciated. It is important that your child recognize the gift and the person who gave it. Gift giving has been a part of celebrations all the way back to The Three Wise Men and beyond. So let the tradition continue.

While preparing for the party, also have your child practice some birthday party etiquette such as what to say when handed a gift. It is always appropriate to say "thank you" while looking at the gift giver. Regardless of what the gift is or if it is something wanted or liked, the act of giving is being acknowledged.

Being thankful for a gift is recognizing the act of giving

The gift may be something your child already has or does not like. Assist the child in preparing responses for such a situation, such as, "Thank you so much for giving this to me." Your child is learning to thank the person for their act of kindness. They are respecting the person, not the gift.

Another scenario might be your child receives two of the same gift. A possible response could be, "You really know what I like. Thanks!" Be aware it is never the giver's responsibility to return a gift or substitute a different one. These situations teach skills that will be used for life.

Opening gifts at the party validates the process that people have gone through to carefully select them. Sometimes it is the joy of watching the child open and like the gift, that makes the present special. With only a few children at the party, this process will not take very long and it can be very enjoyable.

Here are a few methods:

- Parent can hand the gift to the birthday child as others watch.

- Guest can select their gift and hand it to the birthday child.

- The birthday child and gift giver sit next to one another as the gift is being opened.

- Place the gifts in a circle and have the givers sit near their gift.

- Take a photo of the birthday child and guest as the gift is being presented. This could be used as a thank-you card.

Guests can interact as the child is opening presents. They can try to guess what is inside, and the opened gifts can be passed around so all can take a close-up look. Leaving the protective outer wrap on the gifts until after the guests go home will help prevent losing small pieces.

> Leaving the protective outer wrap on the gifts until after the guests go home will help prevent losing small pieces.

As the child opens the gift, they should look at the friend and say thank you. The gifts can then be put away, to be played with after the party. It might be difficult to expect the birthday child to share their new toys at the party.

If gifts are delivered in advance of the party and the giver isn't attending, open those gifts at a time when your child can call and thank them. Think of the time when a friend enthusiastically gave you a gift because they felt it was something you would enjoy. Often, the giver can receive just as much joy as the receiver.

Days before the party discuss with your child what will happen to the gifts after they are opened. Some children want to play with them right away, and some dread having to share them with everyone. Eliminate those fears by explaining the gifts will be shown to the children and then put away until after the party. Also discuss the need to write down what gifts came from each child. If old enough to read, have them repeat the name of the gift giver so that someone can write it down on the guest list. A backup plan is to tape the giver's gift card onto the unwrapped opened gift.

> If gifts are delivered in advance of the party and the giver isn't attending, open those gifts at a time when your child can call and thank them.

After opening each gift the birthday child could give a little goodie bag to each friend as a little thank-you. This shouldn't take the place of a thank-you card in the mail, but might give a reluctant giver a little something, at that moment in time, when letting go might be difficult. It is never too early for children to learn that giving is a nice thing to do for a friend! Gift opening can be done just after snack or meal time. The children are content and calm after eating.

If you do not want gifts, add that to your invitation. Be aware that some guests will disregard your suggestion and arrive with a present. This is the only time we suggest not opening a gift at the party. The gift can discreetly be put it away for a later time.

Winning and losing

Behavior when winning or losing can enrich or offend. Boastful winners can create avoidable awkwardness at a party. Bragging by winners can bring a feeling of defeat to the losers. A group round of applause lead by the parent leader can control the amount of time and attention given to winners. A positive group cheer raises self-esteem far more than boasting.

Life is full of celebrations

The birthday party should be the completion of a time spent planning and anticipating. Weeks are spent preparing for a few hours of celebration, and the anticipation, along with the planning and preparing, are vivid parts of the experience for all involved. Remember your own childhood experiences. Help your child to realize that anticipation, participation, and the memories are all parts of the process.

The birthday party celebration evolves as children grow-up. The event moves from family gatherings, to parties inviting boys and girls, to single sex parties, (sleep over, pizza and DVD's, camp outs, etc.) to coed parties. As your child matures they will have more input into the party planning process.

Setting the Scene

Organizing and Party Safety

Arrangement of the home: Plan what rooms will be used for the party and which rooms are out of bounds. Prepare your child of these decisions so they know what will be expected. For example, open spaces should be available for high-energy activities; table or flat surfaces should be available for projects and eating. You may need to move furniture to the side or rearrange the room for the party.

Your child's room: Encourage your child to put toys safely away and out of sight. This can avert the problem of sharing and worries about broken toys. This could also be a great time, while putting toys away for you and your child to clean out and organize them. If your child's room is a distance from the party area or shared with a sibling then a decision should be made, in advance, about taking guests to their bedroom.

It is always a good idea to do a run-through of the activities. Have your child help you with planning and trying out the activities. Practice all games and projects to be sure you have all items needed and that your child knows exactly how everything will be done. Have your child make any project in advance, to discover if it is too difficult, or if more items are needed, it takes longer to complete, or isn't what was expected. The extra project done, in advance, by your child can be a "sample."

This will build your child's confidence and help you to know how long the activities will take. When your child is familiar with the games and activities, they can take a leadership role and help others. The birthday party is supposed to be a fun time, a celebration. Have fun in the planning and enjoy experimenting along with your child. You are making great memories together.

Establishing a tradition of preparing for the party together when your child is young will assist in future communication. Your child will grow up knowing the routine and, later in childhood, will accept cooperative planning as a family tradition.

Set up areas for the different activities. Have your child help you set the party table. You can use name place cards to assign places or allow the guests to seat themselves. If you are decorating the house do it in advance so that you can enjoy the fruits of your labor and take photos.

Safety

Creating a successful party includes being prepared and ready to adapt. Keeping children safe, happy, and engaged in activities is the goal. Specific safety tips follow.

The number one rule is adult supervision of children at all times. We suggest that at least two adults be present during the party. It has been our experience having two adults per five children is an efficient and safe ratio. With six to ten children have another adult, increase the child adult ratio for every five children. If one adult is preparing an activity or food, another adult is always with the guests. Never assume a group of children will be safe for even a few seconds.

> Never leave children unattended.

Safety tips

- A first-aid kit readily available.

- Bandages are a must have.

- Cool pack in the freezer or ice wrapped in a plastic bag with a towel around, good for bumps.

- Dish towels or paper towels for unexpected cleanups.

- Tissues

- List of parents' contact information. Keep the list nearby on a white board or sticky notes, and readily available so you won't need to search for it in an emergency.

> You might want to think about liability insurance incase a football is kicked into a neighbor's window or a guest gets injured tripping on your rug!

- Keep all family pets separated from the party guests. No matter how friendly the pet, not all children respond kindly to animals.

- Find out before the party of any food allergies and plan accordingly. Allergies should be written on the RSVP list.

- Plan what rooms will be used for the party, and be sure your child knows the boundaries. Let the guests know where to find the bathroom and what rooms can be used. A basement or cleaned garage can be great party rooms.

- Have envelopes or plastic bags available for those surprise items such as a lost tooth, popped button, or dirty clothes. Put the child's name on the bag or envelope before dropping in the item.

- Make sure there are no cords, loose rugs or things that might cause a child to trip and fall.

- If using the outside, take extra care to have no standing water, tools or sharp objects.

- Swimming pool gates should be closed and locked. Pools are off limits for young children who can't swim. You must have a designated watcher of the pool if there is a possibility that a child could fall in the water. Keep chairs or anything else a child could climb on to go over the fence removed from the area.

Pool safety is serious business

- Go over rules of an activity, so children play in a safe manner.

Remind children that running is appropriate when playing games, but not for most inside activities.

Party Management Techniques

The more organized and planned a party is, the less opportunity for chaos. When all the children are occupied with fun and exciting activities they won't be getting themselves and others into trouble.

Keep the party positive with a few helpful hints

- Introduce yourself to the children using your formal name: Mrs Doyle or Miss Georgia. This small formality reminds the children who the leaders are, and prompts them to be respectful.

- To focus the children's attention, start by having them sit down, leaving space between themselves and their neighbors. To bring their attention to you, try this technique. Have them follow your verbal directions, asking everyone to look up, then look down, then look to the right, look at their hands, and now look at me! Or try saying "1-2-3, all eyes on me."

- Another method is ask the children to follow a pattern of clapping hands, such as two claps, one snap, and repeat. For more active children tell everyone to stomp a foot, clap their hands, nod their head, shake their hands, run in place, hop on one foot and keep going until they get some of the wiggles out. Then say, "sit down and listen carefully so you will be able to do the next really fun thing." Speaking in a quiet voice will also keep children's attention.

Ways to talk to the group

A child's brain tends to cancel negative terms used in statements. The mind will grasp "run in the house" rather than "don't run in the house," or "slam the door" instead of "do not slam the door." Restating desired behaviors into a statement such as, "We are going to stay together. Please put your hands in your lap," will produce the expected behavior. When using a statement with a negative, we actually direct their attention to the opposite behavior. "Don't eat with your hands" has just given the child a great idea, while "Please use the fork to eat" makes a statement.

> A child's brain tends to cancel negative terms used in statements. "Don't eat with your hands" has just given the child a great idea, while "Please use the fork to eat" makes a statement.

Explaining the plan, while using positive statements, will set the stage for the party. "We are all going to have a lot of fun today. We all need to know a few rules so we all can enjoy the party. Safety is important. Please remember to walk from place to place, stay with the group, use tools carefully, and remember to keep a little space between you and the person next to you when sitting and standing."

Children need to adjust when moving from one activity to another. Give them time to prepare to change activities. Try stating it this way: "We are going to finish up this art project in five minutes" or "When the buzzer goes off it is time to clean up. You can put it here for now, finish it later and take it home." "In five minutes we need to clean up this area. We need this space for another fun activity." One simple statement is sometimes all that is needed. If the children are actively engaged, you may need to repeat the simple statement.

Another way to get the children's attention is by playing music. The music will stimulate the children while cleaning up or shifting activities.

Having areas set up can be both stimulating and distracting. If you have goodies in sight, they become a temptation. To avoid an impulsive start without directions, or the discovery of hidden objects, remind the children which rooms are available to them during each part of the party.

Dealing with a disruptive child

Sometimes there is one child who has the ability to steer the group towards chaos and bedlam. If you can identify that child in advance, ask them to assist you in showing the group how to do something, or put them in charge of turning on and off the music or some other simple yet important task. Keeping an eye on that child and

Before you discipline another person's child, think about how you would want your child treated. You do not need to confront the child, question or embarrass; you really want to remove the child from the situation so the party can continue.

noting their attention span will help you become aware of when the rest of the group may soon stray. Redirect the activity if children seem to be losing interest. Be ready to stop the activity and move on to another. It is always great to have a plan B. It is important to remain calm and try different ways to keep the children following directions.

You may need to calm a child who has continuing conflicts with others. Avoid drawing attention to the child, because this could escalate the situation and give the child additional attention for negative behavior.

Try one of these:

- Calmly walk over to the child and quietly take their hand and walk them into another room.

- Remove the child from the stimulus of the other children, activities, decorations, and noises, which is usually enough.

- Look at the child, speak in a composed voice and say, "Come with me. We need a moment in the kitchen." Then sit them down. You may suggest a glass of water, or simply say nothing and let the child calm down.

- Ask the child if they are feeling sick or uncomfortable. A child with even a slight fever can be out of sorts.

- No need for a head-to-head confrontation. Do not ask for explanations or excuses. Rather, state the expected behavior: "We pass our food," "We use tools for the job intended," "We stay inside with the other children," "We keep our hands to ourselves."

Then when things are calm, tell the child you are ready to return to the party because you want to rejoin the fun. Ask them if they are ready to return. If they say yes, smile and go back to the party. If they say no, do not leave them unattended. In most situations, within minutes the child will be eager to return. If they do not want to rejoin the party, let them know you understand they are not happy following your rules and you will call their parent. Often the mention of that changes their behavior. Or there could be a concern or health issue you know nothing about. You have a party to host. Ask the child if they want to talk to their parent. This could solve the problem.

Sometimes even with the best of planning, the birthday party parent is surprised to discover their own child is the one who misbehaves. Use the same techniques you would use for other children when dealing with your own. Handling the situation in private will avoid embarrassment for your child. Ask another adult to kindly assist your child as you attend to the group.

When your child actively participates in the party planning from the beginning it will help balance their need for attention at their party.

> Remember to compliment children as they follow expectations. They will feel successful when praised, creating a positive experience for everyone.

8

Family Traditions

You can start some family traditions right now.

Create a:

- Tablecloth that can be signed by the party guests. Use it year after year, adding new signatures.

- Birthday pillowcase that your child can use during their birthday week.

- Special birthday plate for birthday meals.

- Birthday book that can be signed each year.

- Scrapbook birthday book with pictures to be added to each year.

- Measuring spot on a wall or door jamb to record your child's height on their birthday.

- Memory box using a shoe box or other container with memories of the past year. Include photos, copies of favorite art work, pictures of events, and mementos of trips or items collected during the year. Have child write a letter to his or her future self, draw a picture,  or just sign their name. The box could also include a toy, a newspaper, or a postage stamp. Labeled with the date created and the date to be opened for future enjoyment. It is a time capsule of your child's life. It can be opened and resealed, or select special occasions such as entering junior high, graduating eighth grade, becoming a teenager. In the years ahead, this would make a great college graduation gift.

- Decoration for your child's door.

- Tradition of singing "Happy Birthday" as many times as your child is old.

- Tradition of allowing your child to choose their favorite food and birthday cake.

- Photo opportunity: Have your child pose for a birthday photo in the same place every year. Take a picture of your child back-to-back with mom or dad to show how much they have grown. Take a birthday picture each year: Pose your child wearing a man's long sleeved shirt. Yes, the first few years the shirt will be way too big: as the child grows, it will be fun to see the changes.

- Video Opportunity: Create a birthday video using favorite memories from the year and a favorite song. It can be emailed to family and friends on your child's birthday.

Something to consider

The birthday party could be held before your child's actual birthday. The child could then look forward to additional fun celebrating some of these traditions with family on their birthday.

Memory box

A personal time capsule might include other items such as a postage stamp, coins, photos, an ad from the paper, magazine or Internet, etc.

My name is _____

Date _____ I am _____years old.

Write a letter to your future self. Include some of these questions and tell your future self why you like or dislike different things.

My favorite things to do are _____

My favorite color is_____

I love to eat_____

People in my family _____

I have a pet_____ named _____

My favorite toy_____

My hobbies are _____

My favorite sports_____

In 10 years I will be _____

When I grow up I want to be _____

My hair color:_____Height:_____Shoe size: _____

Attached is a drawing of my family.

9

Moment by Moment Party Plan Timeline

Guide for success

The decorations are up, the games and activities are organized, the food is prepared, the house is party ready, the table is set, and your chid knows what to expect. You are ready for a successful and fun party.

> When your child actively participates in the party planning from the beginning it will help balance their need for giving and getting attention at their party.

Welcoming activities *(The first 10 minutes)*

Parent and child greet and welcome guests. Confirm parents contact information. The additional adult will work with children doing a quiet open-ended activity until all children arrive. An open-ended activity is one that allows a child to play without structure or having to finish, such as blocks, making a name tag, puzzles, coloring, paper cutting and gluing, trucks, cars, dolls, stringing beads, etc.

Set the theme *(10-15 minutes)*

Gather the children for introductions. Introduce yourself and all assistants to the children. Establish how you want the children to identify you. For example, "I am Mrs. Doyle, Miss Penny, or I am Andrew's mom." This is important because you are the authority at the party and the children need to be respectful and know who to look to for help and ask questions. Have the children introduce themselves to one another. If the children are sitting in a circle they can pass and hold a soft ball or toy while introduce themselves.

Discuss the overview plan of the party and your expectations. Show a short DVD or read a story. Tell the guests what they are going to be doing. Children are familiar with teachers giving them objectives, so they will feel comfortable knowing what is planned. An objective tells the children the who, what, where, and when of what they will be doing or what is expected of them.

> If the children are still enjoying an activity there is no need to transition to the next activity.

This would be a time to let them know where the bathroom is, to ease any anxiety of a child unfamiliar with your home.

Activities, games, crafts *(30-45 minutes)*

Choose an active game or activity to get the party going. Too many high-activity games can over stimulate and wear out the guests, just as too many quiet activities can bring on fidgety behavior. Common children's activities and games become fun in the new environment of the party. We suggest having two activities ready for each 30-45 minute time slot. If the children are enjoying an activity there is no need to transition to the next activity if they are not ready. Give the children a 5 minute warning, if they sincerely protest stopping, let them continue, wait, then give another warning in 5 more minutes. There is no need to stop the fun.

Doing a craft activity early in the party allows for drying time before the next step or going home. If materials for the activity are set up in front of the children, they will touch them and possibly start before directions are completed. To avoid the distraction, cover the items with a light cloth. Give the directions, showing the sample, and with dramatic flair remove the sheet.

It is always better to over-plan than under-plan. There is nothing like the feeling of having little faces looking up to you asking what's next, and you have run out of ideas! Select at least two options for the first 30 minutes. Stop an unsuccessful game and start another if you realize it is too difficult or the children are not interested. If the game is not working, admit it, tell the children and move on to another. The children will understand.

Some children would rather not play in organized games, so be flexible. You could redirect them, offering another activity or even let them sit it out until ready to participate.

Snack time *(20 minutes)*

Serve a snack, meal, and birthday cake. Have a method for washing hands before eating. If you want the children to sit at a table and wait to be given their food, have something for them to do meanwhile, such as passing vegetables or crackers, party horns, or a toy to play with.

Open gifts *(20 minutes)*

Here are few ways to open the gifts.

- Parent can hand the gift to the birthday child as others watch.

- Guests can select their gifts and hand it to the birthday child.

- Birthday child and giver sit next to one another as the gift is opened.

- Place the gifts in a circle and have the child sit near their gift.

- Take a photo of the birthday child and guest as gifts are opened. This could be used as a thank-you card.

> Ask a parent or friend who enjoys taking photos to be in charge of capturing the great party moments.

Activities and games *(15 – 30 minutes)*

Select an active game after the children have been sitting watching the gifts being opened.

10-minute warning *(Last 10 minutes)*

Remind the children it is almost time for their parents to arrive. The children will not be surprised then when the party is almost over.

Use this time in a number of ways:

- A calm activity helps to prepare them for departing.

- Return to one of the successful activities that the children really enjoyed.

- Allow the children to complete any unfinished projects.

- Read a story.

- Show DVD made during the party for them to enjoy.

- Make sure all the children's things are ready to go home.

- Take a group photo.

If parents arrive early, they can observe the party in action. Final activities also allow the child of the tardy parent to have something to do and not worry or feel uncomfortable while waiting.

Recall with the children the fun things they did at the party, so they go home remembering their good time.

When the parents pick up, have the birthday child say good-bye and thank you for coming. Have your child look at the guest and say, "Thank you for coming to my party."

Let your child know they are to walk their guests to the door when leaving. With both you and your child at the door be assured all children depart with the correct adult and are thanked for attending the party.

Visual timeline

Create a timeline using words and pictures, and show it at the "set the theme" period. This let's children know the plan for the party. It may help eliminate fears.

Picture clues on the timeline will help the non-reader. The visual or word clues on detachable notes can be removed when each activity is over, a big help for the parent and assistant who might forget during the lively activities what's next on the schedule. It is also a good visual reminder for children.

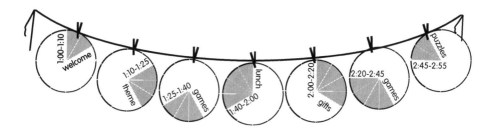

Post-party

Now that the party is over, allow time for your child to play with their new toys. Avoid planning an activity that would take them away from this fun time. Children have a hard time waiting. They will have an expectation that they will get to play with their new toys even though their buddies have left.

Thank-you notes

Guests appreciate getting personalized thank-you notes, whether hand delivered, emailed, or sent through the post office. You can take pictures of each child attending and use the photo to create a thank-you note. It can be as simple as writing on the back of the picture, or writing on a note card.

Thank-you note example:

Dear —————,

Thank you for coming to my party. We had a fun time! I like my (describe the gift).

Sincerely,

(Child signature)

Take into account the attention span of your child. For children who are not yet writing, give them a colorful crayon to "sign" their name. Scribbles are always cherished by family. Discuss the gift and what they may want to say about it and have them sign. This is good preparation for future thank-you note writing. It is also a great time to re-experience the fun of the party.

Thank-you notes can be written within the week, the sooner the better. You might want to make it a game; put envelopes with each guest's name and address in a bag. Have your child, without looking, pull out one of the addressed envelopes and write that thank-you note.

Continue this game until all notes are written. It may take one or more days to complete the process. This is a life skill. Keep it positive, light-hearted, and fun, not a chore. You can use a picture of the guest taken at the party as the note card and have a young child simply write thanks and their name on the back. Parents always appreciate a picture of their child. Mail all the thank-you notes at the same time, so the notes will arrive about the same time.

Use this book as a resource, make notes, add your own ideas, scribble in the margins, and take pictures of your parties as reminders for your future planning. Be confident that creating a plan will produce an organized and successful party

Please share your ideas and comments on our website
www.LibbyandPenny.com or
e-mail us at LibbyandPenny@cox.net or
Like Libby and Penny on Facebook.

Template for Creating a Party

Invitation Plan

Theme: _____

The birthday person is turning _____ *years old.*

The number of guests invited _____

Create the invitation:

- Child's name
- Time
- Date
- Where: address, map if necessary

- Please reply/RSVP: Respond by date with contact number.
- Mention special items or clothing if needed.

- *Decorations: Setting the scene* _____

Birthday party plan

Welcoming activity *(about 10 minutes)*

While waiting for everyone to arrive._____

Set the theme: Party overview and introductions
(optional 10-15 minutes)

Write down what you plan to do:_____

Activities and games *(allow 10 to 15 minutes per game; plan on 30 to 45 minutes total)*

1._____

2._____

Materials needed:

Menu for meal or snack *(allow 20 minutes)*

List foods to be served._____

_____

_____

_____

_____

Food needed:_____

_____

Open gifts *(allow 20 minutes)*
Have your camera ready.

Activities *(15-30 minutes)*
An active game or finish projects.

1._____

2._____

Materials needed_____

End of party *(10 minutes before parent pick-up time)*
1._____

2._____

Materials needed:_____

Be sure guests have goodie bags and everything they came with.

When a guest is ready to leave they should be walked to the door. With many busy children this can be difficult. Discuss, in advance, with your child the plan for thanking the guests and being at the door with you. Have at least one adult remain with the rest of the group.

Observe that each child goes home with expected adult.

The First Birthday Party

A Family Gathering Celebration

Create a double-sided invite by cutting out the white area to create a photo frame and glue to the back of the invite. It will be a great family memento!

Choosing a theme might be similar to the traditional party.

Decorate with balloons at the front door or mailbox to let everyone know where the celebration will be.

Day of the party plan

Welcoming activity

Set aside areas with items the children can enjoy, such as blocks, crayons, paper, play clay, push and pull toys, farm barn, portable doll house, dolls, sorting toys, and play food. Select only a few items to set out; too many choices can be overwhelming. Be sure all areas used by children have adult supervision.

Activities and games for the family

- **Bubbles:** Create an area for playing with bubbles, spilled solution can become slippery. Have an assortment of numerous bubbles, bubble wands, bubble machines, bubble shooters, and bubble bottles with wands. Have enough for all the children. Prepare a solution of soap bubble to refill the spilled or used

containers. This activity is great before snack time: you can be sure all hands will be clean.

Materials needed: Bubbles, bubble solution (1 cup dish soap, 3-4 tablespoons glycerin, and 3-4 cups water), tarp or towels to protect area

- *Bead threading:* use colored shoelaces for threading the beads, and remember to knot one end. Beads can be presorted in packages or set out in a few boxes.

- *Materials needed:* shoelaces, large-holed beads, containers for beads.

- *Family hand or foot T-shirt:* supply a T-shirt for each child attending. Each family member paints their hand or foot and leaves a print of it on the shirt. Whether using hands or feet, comparing and recognizing the different sizes is great fun.

- *Family hand or foot banner:* Use above directions using a large bed sheet, cotton fabric, or white paper. Have permanent pens available for everyone to sign their name next to their imprint. Add liquid dish soap to the tempera paint for easy hands and feet clean-up.

  Materials needed:
  - Cotton t-shirts
  - Fabric or sheet
  - Roll of paper, fabric or tempera paint
  - Containers for paints
  - Plastic table cloth or tarp for project area
  - Use foam rollers or brushes to paint bottom of family members' feet

Meal or snack

Serve favorite bite size foods that one-year olds can eat. Provide cake for the guests and a special cake for the birthday child to enjoy. Now is a great time for those memorable birthday cake eating photos. Families sit all together at one table or you can set up multiple eating areas.

Open gifts

Young children have a limited attention span, and opening many gifts will exceed it. The child may have more fun with the fancy bows and paper than with the gift. The gift giver can help open the gift if the birthday child loses interest. Opening gifts will be of interest to some older children, while the young child may need to be redirected to an area to play. If you indicated no gifts, you need not open any unexpected gifts until after the party.

Outdoor activity

Playing outdoors: outdoor toys: tricycles, scooters, slides, beach balls, swings, jump ropes, and chalk

Safety is important when children of multiple ages are playing in the same space. Playground cones can be used for outlining the area exposed to swinging legs around a swing set. This is a visual clue to both the children and the parents watching from a short distance. Playing ball should be at a distance from toddlers' areas. These cones can also be used for outlining areas and for games.

End of party

Saving the birthday cake for a grand finale can signal the party is coming to the end. Like the wedding tradition. cutting the cake indicates people are then free to depart. Family members can be asked to help clean up and restore order as a welcome form of support.

The Preschool Birthday Party

You are invited

Campbell is turning 4 years old

May 23
4:00 pm
123 ABC Street
Fun Town, USA

Please RSVP by May 18th
000-0000
email

Sample Ave.

123rd Street

ABC Street

Use your child's hand print on the invite and have them number the fingers to show how old they are going to be.

Make an extra one to keep in a memory box!

Preschool Birthday Party plan

Be sure to get a count of how many children from each family will be attending as well as their ages. Confirm if a parent will be attending. Be sure a parent is staying if they intend to bring siblings of the invited guest.

Welcoming activity
(about 10 – 15 minutes)

- Decorate a nametag. Supply string, ribbon, cording, colored markers, stickers, and prepunched cardboard rectangles for writing their names. Encourage everyone to decorate and put on their nametag.

Set the theme *(5-10 minutes)*

Gather the children for introductions, starting with yourself. Establish how you want the children to identify you. For example, "I am Mrs. Doyle, Miss Penny, I am Andrew's mom."

Tell the guests what they are going to be doing. If you selected a theme, be sure everyone understands. Read a short story or show a DVD on the subject. This would be a time to let everyone know what rooms will be used and where the bathroom is located.

Tell the children about the activities and show examples so both the parents and children know what to expect. Explain where the areas are set up and that they can start where they wish. Plan to complete a few of the activities before break time.

Activities *(About 30 minutes)*

The children will enjoy going from area to area with their parent. Make a handout of all the possible activities.

> ### Party Activities:
>
> Select an activity and move at your own pace from area to area.
>
> 30-40 minutes total:
>
> **Watercolor drawing** – beige drop cloth.
>
> **Puzzles** – table.
>
> **Build a block tower** – who can build the tallest? – red blanket.
>
> **Special project related with theme** – table with blue cloth.
>
> **Build your own cupcake** – kitchen – hand washing available.
>
> **Dress up** – long mirror – camera is available for taking pictures.
>
> **Make a puppet table** – green area.

It is helpful to make a list of activities and locations for everyone to know what they can do during the party.

Meal or snack time

A 5-minute warning will be given for completing projects and hand washing. Meet at the table. Food should be age appropriate, easy to prepare and healthy. Serve the birthday cake after the meal or as with the family gathering, as a grand finale.

Open gifts

Group activity *(about 20 minutes)*

- Sing songs, dance (Hokey-Pokey) or finish activities from earlier.

Outdoor Activity *(10 – 15 minutes)*

Free play with parents observing.

End of party *(Last 5 – 10 minutes)*

Gather everyone together to indicate the party is coming to an end. Show the DVD/video made during the party, thank them for coming, remind them of what activities they did, and be sure children have all items they made during the party. Be sure to take photos of all attending.

An organized age-based party will be orderly and easy to keep under control.

13

Traditional Birthday Party

You're invited to a **Birthday Party!**

Doug is turning 12

July 31 • 2:30 pm

123 ABC Street
Fun Town, USA

Please reply/RSVP
July 23
to 000-000-0000
or email

> The birthday person is turning _____ years old.
>
> The number of guests invited: _____

Decorations

A few balloons by the door, a colorful poster with the birthday child's name, party hats and party horns can set the theme. The children will be enthusiastic being in a new environment.

Traditional Birthday Party plan

Welcoming activity *(about 10 minutes)*

Select an activity:

- *Surprise balls* are colorful balls made of crepe paper strips wrapped in layers around small gifts. When unwrapped the toys are revealed as the layers are removed. The children will make surprise ball using long strips of crepe paper that will be wrapped around a small ball or plastic egg.

- *How to make a surprise ball:*

    - *Give each child a container with a number of small toys to be wrapped.*

– *Start with a plastic egg filled with a toy, a small ball or a yoyo. Wrap using crepe paper strips around the center item securing the first strip with tape.*

– *After a few layers insert a balloon, small toy, fake mustache, small charm, gum, candy, or sticker to the next layer, wrapping until all toys in their containers are wrapped inside the surprise ball.*

– *The ball may become lumpy. The balls will all have the same items, but will not be in the same order so, when exchanged, each child will have the surprise of discovery. The fun of this activity is in assembling the balls and interacting with one another while doing it. Young children may want the one they made, so write their names on the outside.*

• ***Decorate a goodie bag:*** Have each child write their name on a bag and decorate using markers, glitter, stickers, etc. They can put all their goodies in this bag during the party.

• ***Cereal necklaces:*** In advance cut elastic cord or yarn long enough to easily go over a child's head. Knot one end and dip the other in white glue. The hardened glue works like a needle. Have small containers of colored oat cereal for each child to string a necklace. The children can create a pattern stringing the O-shaped oat cereal. This becomes a snack during the party. Using containers for each child is a sanitary way to avoid multiple hands in one container.

Items needed: Elastic cording, yarn or string, white glue, oat cereal, containers for each child's O-shaped oat cereal.

Set the theme *(optional 15 – 20 minutes)*

- Read a story about a birthday party. Share a short family story about a birthday party. Explain what the plans are for the party.

- Children are familiar with teachers giving them objectives so they will feel comfortable knowing what is planned.

Activities and games *(allow 10 – 15 minutes per game; plan 30 minutes total)*

Balance the games between high and low activity. You know your child's attention span; base the timing on what you know. Older children can concentrate longer on one game or activity.

- *Team relay games:* Divide the children into two groups. Use playground cones to identify boundary.

  - *Pillowcase (sack) race:* The child puts both feet into the pillowcase and hops from the starting line to finish as fast as they can go.

  - *Wheelbarrow race:* One child picks up another by the ankles and they walk in that position to a line, switch positions, and return to start line. This may be difficult for young children to do.

  - *Potato races (or use marshmallows):* Each team has a spoon and a potato, and each child will carry the potato on the spoon to the line and back without dropping it. If they drop it, either start over or have them pick it up and continue to finish line.

- *Hula hoop:* See how long the children can keep the hoop twirling. Have one hoop for each child.

- *Bean bag toss:* Toss bean bags through a hole in a board, assigning points for each successful toss.

- *Jacks:* Have children sit on the floor for this game. A number of jacks are dropped on the floor and the child tosses a ball in the air, while picking up as many jacks as they can. Or start by picking up one per toss, then two per toss, then three, etc.

- *Giggle scarf:* Children sit in circle, someone tosses a scarf up, and children are to giggle until scarf hits the ground, then must stop. Whoever keeps giggling must be the scarf-tosser in the new round.

Arts and crafts

- *Create puppets:* Puppets can be made out of paper bags, socks, mittens, a finger from a glove, your own fingers, etc. Decorating with many materials: scraps of felt, fabric, marking pens, scrapbook papers, buttons, pipe cleaners, yarn, Popsicle sticks, needle and thread (older children) wire, markers, Styrofoam ball, glue, etc. Have scissors and glue available.

  Create a stage by draping an old sheet over a table. Cut a rectangle hole for the stage area. Have the children take turns being on stage (under the table). Or use a big box, large enough for children to fit in, cut a hole for the stage.

- *Create musical instruments:*

  - *Make a little guitar*: Use small boxes and cover with rubber bands for plucking.

– ***Make a tambourine***: Decorate outside of two plates using stickers, markers, ribbon, etc. Tape or staple two paper plates together, first putting rice or beans in between them..

– ***Music jar***: Partially fill a plastic jar with beans, coins, beads or stones. Decorate outside of jar with string or ribbon. Shake it to the music!

Menu for meal or snack *(allow 20 minutes)*

Sit at dining table and have small decorated cups filled with nuts and raisins (snack mix) by each place setting. Pass out the surprise balls to unwind. Have party hats and party horns. Children can snack on nuts and raisins while waiting for the meal. Prepare in advance traditional foods such as macaroni and cheese, peanut butter on celery, carrots, turkey pita wrap, English muffin pizza, salad, grapes and berries. End with cake and ice cream.

Open gifts *(15-20 minutes) Refer to chapter 5*

Opening gifts is an excellent low energy activity after eating.

An active game will work well now *(20 minutes)*

Simon says: One person becomes Simon and gives directions to the other children. Each statement the children follow are prefaced with the words "Simon says" such as "Simon says jump on one foot, Simon says tap your head, and Simon says clap hands." Children are eliminated by not responding when hearing Simon says or they respond when the words Simon says, were not used before a statement. Simon quickly gives commands for the children to follow, then Simon gives a command without saying Simon Says, the children who respond are eliminated. The last child still in the game becomes Simon.

Calm end of party activities *(allow 15 minutes)*

- *Remember items on the tray game.* Place a
  number of items on a tray. Have the children look
  at them. Tell them you are going to remove the tray
  and they can try to remember what was on the tray.
  Remove or cover the tray with a cloth. Give the
  children paper and pencils. Have then write or draw
  as many items as they remember. See who did the
  best, work in teams, give a prize to the highest number
  remembered. For young children cover the tray and
  have them tell what they remember seeing. Bring out
  the object to show they are correct.

  – *Option 2*: Show the tray again, turn around remove
    an item, turn back and see who remembers what
    was taken. Keep playing as long as they are having
    fun. Possibly have a guest do the take away
    process just for the fun of it.

- *What is this?* Show the children unique objects and
  have them guess what they are and how they were
  used. For example an old fashioned apple peeler, allow
  the children to ask yes or no questions to discover
  what the item is or its use.

  *Ideas: hair roller, doilies, roller skate key, a record, unique
  kitchen tools, old belt buckle, apple corer, lunch box,
  coasters, floppy disc, and shower cap.*

End of party

It is a good idea to have a calm organized activity under
way when the parents arrive.

Be sure guests have goodie bags, everything they came
with and depart with expected adult.

When a guest leaves they should be walked to the door. With many busy children this can be difficult. Discuss and plan with your child the process of thanking the guests and being at the door with you. Have one adult remain with the rest of the group.

Dinosaur Party

You are invited to a
Dinosaur Birthday Party!!!

Gregory
is turning 7 Years Old!
May 10
2:00 pm
348 Sample Street
Fun Town, USA

Please RSVP by
May 3
000-0000

Invitation can be a plastic egg with the invitation enclosed. Make the invitation using the outlined shape of a dinosaur and fill in the information, including a few stickers for fun.

When your child discovers dinosaurs, be prepared for all things dinosaur! These prehistoric marvels are wondrous and exciting for children.

The birthday person is turning _____ years old.

The number of guests invited _____

Dinosaur Party plan

Decorations: Create a tropical atmosphere using fern and big leaves for decorations. You can create the leaves using large construction paper or crepe-paper. Use what may already be in your child's room for inspiration: books, miniature dinosaurs, and posters. Use the *Dig for Bones plaster-of-Paris rocks* as part of a table centerpiece. The children can select a rock to dig into and discover a hidden dinosaur.

Items needed: Include items you already have and what you may want to buy: pith helmets, binoculars, scarves, plastic dinosaurs, plastic eggs, bags for goodies, plaster of Paris, flat-head screwdriver, small bucket, dirt, rocks, and a few small plants for some activities.

Welcoming activity *(about 10 minutes)*

Sticks and stones: Give each child an elastic cord with a knot on one end. Have small containers of oat cereal, (pretend stones) for each child to string into a necklace. Use licorice twine for the sticks or use as the cord to string the necklace. This becomes a snack for the dinosaur adventurers (Paleontologists) during the party.

Items needed: Elastic cord, oat cereal, licorice twine, licorice pieces, and containers for each child's O shaped oat cereal.

Set the theme *(optional 10 minutes)*

Read a few pages or a short book about dinosaurs or show a short dinosaur video.

Activities and games *(allow 10 to 15 minutes per game; plan on 30 minutes total)*

Give the children the items you purchased to prepare them to become Paleontologists such as pith helmets, binoculars, scarves to tie around their necks (can also be used for gathering up small dinosaurs).

- ***Dinosaur hunt:*** Outdoors, hide small dinosaurs in colored plastic eggs. Assign a color to each child. This allows the children to assist one another in hunting for their eggs. On the count of three the children start to explore the area looking for their dinosaur eggs.

- ***Indoors or limited outdoor space:*** Use a sandbox, or a large under-bed plastic tub filled with sand for dinosaur-bone hunt. Hide small dinosaur figures in the sand. The children can dig using small shovels or spoons. For a more realistic detail hide chicken or turkey bones that have been cleaned in bleach water.

Items needed: Sandbox, small dinosaur figures, pennies, bleached chicken or turkey legs, bags for each child's goodies, shovels or spoons, and colored plastic eggs.

Active structured activity

• *Dinosaur relay:* Divide the children into dinosaur teams such as Brontosauruses, Tyrannosaurus Rexes or Triceratops.

Indoors, divide the children into two groups and have them stand on opposite sides of the room while you set down two large boxes filled with packing material. Inside will be enough eggs for each child plus an extra. Start the hunt relay on the count of three. One child from each team runs to the box, digs in and finds an egg, runs back to the start so the next child can go. The team that finds all their eggs first are the winners. Hide the eggs again and mix up the teams.

If you plan on keeping the eggs, this is the time to gather them up, or if the children are keeping them, put the eggs in a bag with their name on it.

• *Active outdoor*

– *Tyrannosaurus Rex tag:* Select one child to be the ferocious dinosaur or "it" who will catch the other children. When a child is tagged they must stay still until all children are tagged.

– *Option:* Once tyrannosaurus tags a child, the child becomes the new Tyrannosaurus Rex, "it."

- *Active indoor*

  - *Dinosaur jump:* They will all become dinosaurs for this game period. Explain that the idea is to jump over or swim (pretend) through the river, but they have to get out of the river before the music stops. Have the children ready to start, turn on the music and have the dinosaurs cross back and forth and keep crossing. Those caught in the water when the music stops have to sit out the next round. After the second round, the new group of those still in the water sit out for the next round and the children caught the first time go back in. Play for a number of rounds.

  - *Dig for Bones:* An activity older children who can work with a chisel, a flat-head screwdriver; even a cuticle tool will work. The children will dig and dig to unearth treasure.

Make kits in advance for each child using a mixture of sand, stones, and plaster of paris. Add soil to make the plaster less dense and easier to chisel. Use wax paper to line the inside of a small container. Put soil or stones on the wax paper, and fill it halfway with the plaster mixture. Place a dinosaur or other toy that will not be destroyed in the mixture. When the mixture starts to harden, pour in more to fully cover the dinosaur. Then pop the hardened block out of container and use the container again.

Use these rocks with hidden dinosaurs as centerpieces or as a party favor to take home.

Items needed: plaster of paris, tools, plastic dinosaurs, bones and containers to use to make mold.

- Younger children can use a sand box or blow-up child's pool. Bury fossils in the sand (or use shredded paper) and give each child a spoon or small shovel to dig for dinosaurs. You can use real chicken bones, cardboard bones, dog bones, or dog treats.

Open-ended activities

- Dinosaur puzzles on a table.

- Blocks and plastic dinosaurs.

- Play dough with dinosaur cutters, rolling pins, plastic knives or popsicle sticks

Items needed: play dough, or make play dough ahead of party day and keep in plastic bags. This could also be a party favor to be taken home.

Arts and Craft projects

- Create dinosaur environments for the children to take home. A terrarium is a miniature landscape with plants. Provide each child with a small bucket, dirt, rocks, and a few small plants to create an environment for their plastic dinosaurs. Use a glass jar, a plastic soda bottle or a plate.

- Make a dinosaur puppet using an old white sock; glue various materials to the face of the dinosaur. Recycled Styrofoam could be used for spikes, felt or goggles for eyes, yarn for hair. Use fabric glue, and let dry before taking home. Set up a little puppet stage, as simple as an upright box that the kids kneel behind while holding up their puppets. Some can do puppet shows for others.

- *Make dinosaur costume*

    - Dinosaur heads using multiple sized boxes or grocery bags. Precut holes in the bottom to fit over the children's heads. Use duct tape to close the opening. Have a large circle cut in the front to allow for child's face. Add teeth using cut up pieces of sponge and glue onto the face. Create spikes and funny lumps and bumps on the outside of box or bag using paper cone cups, pieces of sponge, recycled paper cups, colored paper and scraps. Either pre-paint boxes and have children add spots, recycled paper cups, colored paper scraps. stripes, or paint themselves.

    - Make big feet using decorated tissue boxes with the bottom cut off. Use the existing slit of the tissue box for the child's foot to slide through and then put on their shoes.

Menu for meal or snack *(allow 20 minutes)*

- Food for the carnivores, meat-eating dinosaurs: little hot dogs or chicken legs.

- Food for the herbivores or plant-eating dinosaurs: celery, carrots, broccoli, ranch dip, berries and beans.

- Green gelatin ice cubes in each container of water could become swampy dinosaur juice.

- Dinosaur cupcakes: Add a plastic dinosaur on top of each cupcake.

- Dessert idea: Turn a gallon of chocolate ice cream upside down and smash it a bit to make it look like a mountain, and add marshmallow fluff to resemble snow.

Open gifts *(allow 20 minutes)*
- Have your camera ready.

Activities *(20 minutes)*
An active game or finishing projects will work well now.

- ***Dinosaur egg toss.*** Teams of two children line up, each pair face to face. Give each team a plastic egg to toss between them. Every time they toss the egg without dropping it they take a step back. The last team that still hasn't dropped its egg is the winner. They can open the egg and have the goodies inside (put in stickers, gummy candies, gum, or nothing.)

- ***Dinosaur ice cube toss.*** Follow the same game directions as the dinosaur egg toss (above) but use ice cubes with dinosaurs frozen inside in place of the eggs. This will need to be prepared before the party day.

End of party *(10 minutes before parent pick-up time)*
Be sure guests have goodie bags, everything they came with and goes home with expected adult.

Be an Artist Party

Be an Artist Party

Its Jackson's
Birthday!!
January 28 • 2:30 pm

123 ABC Street
Fun Town, USA

Please reply/RSVP by Jan 18
to 000-000-0000 or email

We will be painting, so please wear appropriate clothes.

Sample Ave.

123rd Street

ABC Street

Be an Artist party

Jackson Pollack, or select your own favorite artist.

Party plan

Welcoming activity
(about 10 minutes)

- ***Decorate large t-shirts:*** Give each child a large T-shirt to use as painters' smocks and decorate with markers.

- Decorate an apron to wear to protect clothing while painting. Children may enjoy writing their names on the aprons and T-shirts using paint pens, glitter, etc.

- Make a sit-upon. This cushion is made of two pieces of vinyl, heavy paper or card stock. Punch holes around outside edge, add a small stack of newspaper between the vinyl. Tie together using yarn to thread through the holes. The children can kneel or sit on these while painting.

Set the theme *(optional 10-15 minutes)*

- Show a short DVD, read a story, and tell the guests what they are going to be doing. Children are familiar with teachers giving them objectives.

- Show the children a Jackson Pollock painting; explain that they were called action paintings because he walked around, over, and sometimes on his canvases, using the energy of movement to create art.

- If selecting another artist, find out details of their art and use as the premise for the children's art project.

- To get young children in the mood, ask them to show using their hands or whole body what actions they think animals make. Have them imagine what those movements would look like if the animal had a paintbrush!

  – A snake—slither motions.

  – A rabbit—hop, hop, hop.

  – A bee—buzz in a circle.

  – A dog—tail wagging.

  – A bird—flying.

- Listen to music and let the children express how the music makes them feel.

Activities and games *(allow 10 to 15 minutes per game; plan on 30 – 45 minutes total)*

- ***Action painting:*** Write each child's name on the back of a canvas. Lay canvases on tarps covering the floor.

  Have available: buckets of paint, multiple sizes of brushes, string, small rollers, sponges, etc.

  Explain the rules, such as:

  – Be sure to keep the paint on your canvas.

  – Use materials safely—keep a tight hold on your brush.

  – When dripping or splattering be aware of the people next to you. Keep paint on the canvas.

  – The walls in the home are already painted.

- Your canvas is your canvas; assist other people only if they ask.

- Keep the tools with their paint color, and try squeeze bottles.

- Use the wash basin, tub, or can provided for cleanup.

- A few methods for sharing the paint and tools:

  - Give each child a different tool and color of paint.

  - Put on some music and let them create.

  - Remind the children of the different animal actions they discussed earlier to inspire their actions.

  - Once they use the first color and tool, have them pass or trade with another child.

  - The children can select a color and tool, use it on their canvas, and hand it to the next child.

Allow the children time to create. It sometimes takes a while for reluctant a child to get started, but as they watch others, they will get an idea and begin. Remember that fun and creativity are found in the process, not the end product.

- *Decorate wooden frames, boxes, or cardboard frames:* Paint the frames with a light coat of gesso in advance or have children gesso items when they first arrive so it will dry during the rest of the party.

- *Marble painting:* Select cardboard boxes large enough for the size paper you choose. Place paper, dishes of colored paints, and marbles nearby. Write child's name on the back of the paper. Have child select a marble, place marble in a dish with paint. Use a spoon to coat the marble with paint, lift marble out of paint, then place on paper in box lid. Roll marble around to make a design. Remove marble, rinse in soapy water and place in another color. Repeat process until happy with marble painting

Have a place ready for their artwork to dry.

Menu for meal or snack *(allow 20 minutes)*

- *Decorate a pizza to look like Pollock's work.*

- *Decorate a cupcake* using multiple colors of frosting, sprinkles, and colored candies

- *Jell-O gelatin color:* When two of the primary colors are combined they create the secondary colors. Show these color principals in a fun and edible way. In advance of the party, make three recipes of gelatin dessert. One blue (blueberry), one red (strawberry) and one yellow (lemon). Pour each recipe in a different 13 x 9 inch pan sprayed with cooking spray. Cut the slices into 2 inch squares. Place the squares in attractive plies and encourage the guest to take one of each. Explain they are going to be encouraged to play with their food. Select a yellow square hold a red square next to it, what color do they see? Mixing two primary colors such as red and yellow create the secondary color orange. Have the children layer a yellow and blue square to create green. layering red and blue will make purple. Enjoy eating the primary and secondary colors. To make extra firm gelatin squares add an extra package of unflavored gelatin to each color.

Open gifts *(allow 20 minutes)*

Opening gifts is an excellent low energy activity after eating.

Activity *(20 minutes)*

- *Relay races:* Create two teams of children. Each child selects a color. Place slips of colored paper in a box and have each child without looking select a colored slip. When it's their turn they run to a large basket or box to find an object of the same color and run back to the start line. The objects will be somewhat hidden in the basket or box (use recycled paper or packing peanuts). Possible objects: colored crayons, markers, cars, small toys, blocks, colored socks, etc.

- Finishing up any projects can take place now.

End of party

It is a good idea to have a calm organized activity underway when the parents arrive to take their children home. Watching a DVD of the party will bring the party to a enjoyable close.

Be sure guests have goodie bags, everything they came with and go home with the expected adult.

Fancy Dress-Up
Tea Party

Please come to Bella's

Fancy Dress-Up
Tea Party

July 24 • 4:00 pm

123 ABC Street
Fun Town, USA

RSVP by July 14
000-000-0000 or email

Dress in fancy
dress-up party clothes
Hats, gloves and shiny shoes will all be welcome.

Your child can get fancy and embellish the invitation with glitter, buttons, etc., to deliver to their friends. Make each one unique or make color-copies of one!

Fancy Dress-Up Tea Party plan

Welcoming activity *(about 10-15 minutes)*

Think of a fun activity for guests waiting for others to arrive. Select one:

- Decorate a teacup, a special plate, or charger which is placed under a plate for the added beautification and adornment of the table. Decorate the charger plate after writing your name on the back. The charger plate is not used for food so decorate as you wish, stickers, markers, etc.

- Weave a placemat with fancy ribbons to be used for the table setting. Select two sheets of construction paper. Fold one in half (the folded section will be more of a square than a rectangle) keeping it folded start at the fold edge cut leaving about an inch on either side and at the end uncut. Repeat cutting one inch apart, minding not to cut all the way to the end, just an inch short of the edge. For weaving the second piece of construction paper, cut into 1 inch strips. Start weaving the strips of 1 inch paper, move the strips over and under, then over and under again. Start the next strip going under and then over, then under and over until complete. Use a bit of ribbon to add to the exquisiteness of the mat. A dot of glue will keep it together.

Open-ended activities

- Dress-up area have an assortment of hats, jackets, crowns, capes, gloves, shoes, wigs, caps, etc. to try on. Safely set up a mirror. Have a camera ready for some unique shots.
- Puzzle table assorted puzzles

Set the theme *(optional 10 – 15 minutes)*

When the children are ready, read a picture book or story about a tea party, so they will know what to expect. There are excellent examples available today.

Activities and games *(allow 10 – 15 minutes per game plan on 30 minutes total)*

You want to keep the children engaged and involved. An organized age-based party will be orderly and easy to keep under control. Balance the games between high and low activity. Too many high-activity games can overstimulate and wear out the guests, just as too many quiet activities can bring on fidgety behavior. You know your child's attention span: base the timing on that. Older children can concentrate longer on one game or activity.

If you are planning a craft or art activity, scheduling it early allows projects to dry before being taken home.

Activities *(allow 10 – 15 minutes per game plan on 30 minutes total)*

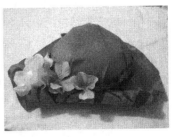

Make a party hat: Have the children decorate with silk flowers, ribbons, lace, tulle, fabric scraps, and or sequins. Tie ribbon around the brim and finish with a tremendously immense bow. Long glamorous dangling ribbons will be most enchanting. Use white glue or with adult supervision use a glue gun..

Party hat
Advance preparation

In advance of the party create a hat for each child using grocery bags or colored construction paper. To form a circle to fit on a child's head find a mixing bowl approximately the size of your child's head. Prepare the construction paper or bag by cutting it into a large enough circle to cover the bowl and create a brim around the edge, then dampen it with warm water. Mold the bag or paper over the mixing bowl, secure the paper until dry using a rubber band. Roll the brim or flatten to dry. Allow to dry overnight, longer if its humid. Paint in advance or keep them their natural color.

Just a caution about glitter: When using glitter show the children how to prepare the area for glittering. Collect low flat boxes to use under the project being glittered to collect fallen glitter. Demonstrate how to select a color of glitter and place it nearby, then squeeze just enough white glue to decorate a section of the hat at a time, put the glue down and gently sprinkle the glitter over the still wet glue. Wait a few moments, tip the hat and shake extra glitter into box. Carefully select the next area to glue and glitter. This might be done outdoors, on a plastic mat where spills won't matter, or over a large box, so the excess is easy to clean up. Kids love this, but also tend to glitter until the glitter container is empty, have enough for each child to enjoy because they may use the whole bottle. Nothing is more surprising to a child than watching all the glitter fall off their project because the glue dried before they added the glitter or there wasn't any glue where they put the glitter.

- *Make jewelry*

  - *Make a necklace or bracelet:* Have beads and string for the children on their own trays so problems with sharing don't arise. That keeps things organized too.

A few tricks when beading. One is to use waxed floss. Another is to use two lengths of cord. Measure the amount of waxed floss or cord to go around the child's neck almost three times. Start by placing a bead or attach a clasp in the middle of the string. This creates two cords to pass through each additional bead. Attach the second bead passing both cords or wax floss through the bead, tie a knot: right over left and left over right, tighten the knot, and add another bead, tie a knot, tighten, etc. This knotting will help keep the beads from falling off. And will look very chic. When the necklace is long enough to be completed add a closing clasps, or be sure the necklace easily slips over the head and tie both ends together in a knot to complete. For young children, be prepared to assist especially when young children are ready to close up the necklace or bracelet. Your local craft store or on line websites will have lots of choices of beads and string.

Macaroni necklace
Advance preparation

To color macaroni combine 1 tablespoon alcohol with a few drops of food coloring in a self sealing plastic bag. Add a hand full of macaroni (20) into the bag. Seal the plastic bag and mix. Remove and dry on paper towels. The alcohol evaporates. The macaroni absorbs color and doesn't get sticky.

– *Macaroni necklaces* can be easily made by young children. Macaroni is much easier to thread.

• *Dance time:* Allow time to turn on music and let the children dance, twirl, and pretend. Give them plenty of room (a patio or large playroom) to move. The garage without cars is a good place too. You could provide tap or ballet shoes or special socks to wear.

• *Practice tying neckties or scarves:* Have a mirror nearby! Use long strips of cotton fabric sewn down the length of the fabric to become a tie. Simply turn in the ends to finish off. If you used a cotton fabric they can be decorated.

Menu for meal or snack *(allow 20 minutes)*

• Drinks served using teapots. Tea, apple juice, or pink lemonade will be fun. Have teapots that children can handle.

• *Serve tea sandwiches without crusts*: Possible suggestions: cucumber and cream cheese, peanut butter and honey, egg salad, or chicken salad. Cut sandwiches in shapes: triangles, circles, use cookie cutters. Place on fancy plates and serve. Add fancy toothpicks for hors d'ouvres.

• Have the children sit down at the table. Assign places using place cards or allow them to select their own spot. Have the children find their charger, a charger is placed about an inch away from the edge of the table with a plate on top. Be sure to have the children wear their fancy hats and jewels to tea. Either pass the sandwiches or set up a buffet. Encourage trying different sandwiches. Be sure to include nuts, berries, raisins, small pieces of vegetables for different eaters.

If including scones you could use jam and butter. The chargers are traditionally removed from the table when serving dessert, yet keeping them there may protect the table cloth. Dessert can be served on a fancy tiered plate with little cupcakes and cookies.

- **_Tea time chat:_** Print up questions and conversation starters to use while eating. What is your favorite color? What is your favorite outdoor activity? Do you have a pet? Do you play a musical instrument? What is your favorite book? What do you like to do when you have nothing to do? How did your parents select your name? If you had 3 wishes what would they be? What is your middle name? How many sisters and brothers do you have? Add your own additional questions.

Open gifts _(allow 20 minutes)_

- Opening gifts is a low energy activity after eating.

Activities _(20 minutes)_

An active game will work well now.

- **_Tea cup hunt:_** Cut out small photos of tea cups and glue onto 2–3 inches circles. Prepare at least 6 times the number of guests attending. Hide in advance of the party. If any are discovered prior to the game smile and say it's a secret. When it is time to hunt for the tea cups give each child a container to hold the cups they find (a goodie bag). Show the children an example of what they will be looking for and what rooms they can find them. Clarify they are to take a cup when they find one and place it in their bag. Once they have found 6, they can then assist the rest of the children hunt. The first to find 6 wins a prize or gets a big round of applause from the group.

- ***Ribbon dancing:*** Attach ribbon to a 15-inch dowel or a 12-inch ruler will do nicely. Have the children dance waving the ribbons.

- ***Build a maypole:*** Build a maypole, using ribbons and a tall pole. Attach long ribbons to top of pole. Have each child hold a loose end, turn on music, and have them walk around the pole wrapping the ribbons around it. Then see if they can unwind the ribbons. They can do this many times if they are enjoying it. Or try weaving the ribbons by alternating over and under.

- Finishing up any projects can also take place now.

It is always a good idea to have a calm organized activity underway when the parents arrive to take their child home. If you are fortunate enough to have had someone videotaping the party, this is a great time for the children to watch themselves before going home. It is also a good time to read or reread a story, or to have them sing some favorite songs.

End of party

Be sure guests have goodie bags and everything they came with. Be sure each child goes home with expected adult Have your child stand at the door with you and thank their friends for coming. After the last friends have left, it is the time to play with the gifts and talk about the fun at the party. Maybe a time for the grandparents to come and hear the stories of the great time that was had.

Be a Chef Cooking Party

Recipe for a Great Birthday Party

Sara is having a Chef's birthday party

May 23
4:00 pm
1941 E Chestnut Street, Fun Town

Please reply/RSVP by
May 18th to 000-0000

Attach a recipe card invitation to a kitchen gadget or a little pizza box with the invitation inside. The invitation can also be a triangle shape resembling a slice of pizza.

Be a Chef Cooking party

Mixing, kneading, baking, adding toppings of choice, what could be more fun? Young chefs between 5 and 13 will enjoy the many facets of this party. The children will make their own pizza, create folded napkin designs, assemble their own cookbooks, and more. Playing is great and playing with your food is that much better.

Birthday plan

Welcoming activity *(about 10 minutes)*

List the activity for guests waiting for others to arrive.

- *Young chefs:* have the children create their own pizza using construction paper for the dough. Place the paper pizza on a square of foil to resemble the tray. Have red watercolors or markers available for the sauce. Use stickers for sausage, pepperoni, mushroom, and green pepper, and cut strips of yellow paper for cheese. Have the children select the kinds of toppings they like on their pizza.

- *Older chefs:* Make recipe books. Set up an area with items to make a recipe book. Fold paper in half, staple or sew to bind or purchase blank books. Have the recipe for the pizza available, and some colorful images to cut out of cooking magazines to decorate the recipe book.

Set the theme *(optional 15 – 20 minutes)*

Tell the chefs they will be receiving their chef uniforms, preparing pizza, folding napkins, setting the table, playing a few games and viewing a video or reading a story about making pizza. Include an explanation of basic health practices incorporate hand washing and the need for working on a clean work surface.

Show a short video, read a story/book, hand out costumes, tell the chefs what the menu is for the party.

Activities and games

1. Set out ingredients so children can start preparing the pizza, after washing their hands.

   Have enough bowls for each guest. Two chefs can work together measuring oil, water, etc.

   Have chefs set out possible toppings for their pizzas, and (according to their age and ability) have them grate cheese or put pre-shredded cheese in dishes.

   Possible toppings: olives, tomatoes, cheese, sausage, pepperoni, mushroom, green pepper, etc.

   Make your own dough the night before for very young chefs or use a store brand of pizza dough. Place each pizza on foil or parchment paper and write the child's name next to it.

Menu for meal or snack *(allow 20 minutes)*
List foods to be served..

Easy pizza
1 package of flour tortillas or English Muffins

1 jar of favorite pizza sauce.

1 package of pizza cheese mozzarella and cheddar

Assorted toppings

Pizza dough recipe:
1 1/2 cups flour

1 teaspoon salt

3/4 teaspoon active dry yeast

1/2 cup lukewarm water (110° temperature)

1 tablespoon olive oil

½ teaspoon sugar

Combine water, sugar, and yeast let set for about 10 minutes. Combine: all dry ingredients, olive oil, including yeast mixture, in a large bowl. Mix with a spoon until well blended. Place the dough on a clean floured surface. Push dough into a ball shape to start the kneading process. Using the heal of the hand push down on the dough and away. Fold the dough in half and press back into a ball shape. Turn the dough a bit, start again, press with the heal of the hand, push down and away, fold back, turn dough and do it again. Continue the process until firm. To test firmness, make a fist, push into the dough, if the dent doesn't remain indented, it is ready to put in a bowl covered with a towel to let rise. It should rise in 10–15 minutes if placed in a warm spot. Dough will rise and almost double in size. With floured hands place dough onto floured surface to roll out using a rolling pin. Top with favorite toppings. Place on lightly greased pan or parchment paper. Write the child's name on the parchment paper. Note: without toppings the dough poofs up. Cook 450 for 20 minutes.

Some games to play while waiting for the pizza to bake.

Chef question-and-answer games, for older chefs.

Divide the chefs into teams. Have the teams guess the answers to some chef and cooking questions.

Why is the toque the traditional chef's hat?

A. To keep the head warm

B. To keep hair from falling into the food

C. To make a fashion statement

Answer: B. The toque (chef's hat) dates back to the 16th century when hats were commonly worn to show one's profession. There is no single known origin of the toque, which is the French name for the hat. One popular story is that a king found a hair in his food. He beheaded the person it belonged to, according to the story, from then on all kitchen staff were ordered to wear hats.

Why is the toque so tall?

A. Some food practices include throwing food from one chef to another so head protection is necessary.

B. It allows chefs to properly store their utensils when not in use.

C. Different heights of hats indicate rank within a kitchen. They also denote how accomplished the chef is.

Answer: C.

Why do chefs' trousers have a hound's-tooth checked pattern on them?

    A. The pattern matches the often used French tablecloths.

    B. Serves to camouflage minor stains.

    C. They were stylish many years ago.

Answer: B. The checked pattern on trousers helps to camouflage food stains.

Why do chefs wear double-breasted reversal jackets?

    A. The cook needs to keep warm when moving from kitchen to the large refrigerated storage rooms.

    B. It can be reversed to hide stains.

    C. The white jacket is a form of camouflage allowing it to blend into the mostly white kitchen equipment.

Answer: B. The double-breasted jacket can be reversed to hide stains. The thick cotton fabric protects the cook from heat and splattering from the stove. Knotted cloth buttons were used because they could be washed often and didn't melt when near hot items.

Is there a reason why there are so many folds in the toque (hat)?

A. They are needed to make the hat stand up.

B. The 100 folds are said to represent the many different ways a chef knows how to cook an egg.

C. The folds were used to hold the customer's bill.

Answer: B. The 100 folds of the toque are supposed to represent the many ways a chef can cook an egg. Folds are like the stripes on a military uniform; they increase with rank or accomplishment. The number of pleats goes up to one hundred, which would be a most accomplished chef.

Why do chefs wear white?

A. White cotton is inexpensive.

B. White reflects heat rather than absorbing it.

C. The use of white for chefs clothing, especially the highly visible chef's hat, is intended to denote cleanliness.

Answer: B.

Who used the first napkins?

A. The Spartans. They were lumps of dough cut into small pieces and rolled and kneaded at the table, a custom that led to using sliced bread to wipe the hands.

B. Cavemen, who used animal fur to wipe their mouths.

C. The Romans. Foot soldiers carried them in their leggings.

Answer: A.

During Roman times the napkin:

A. Was called a mappa and was supplied by each guest. It was filled with leftovers like today's doggy bags.

B. Was a symbol of prestige. Only the wealthy used them

C. Was actually the plate or base used for serving food

Answer: A.

During the Middle Ages:

A. People used a communal napkin or the back of the hand, clothing, or a piece of bread.

B. The handkerchief was invented and took the place of the traditional napkin.

C. The napkin was used on the chair to protect the covering from food spills.

Answer: A.

Napkin game questions

Wrap questions around a napkin or napkin ring. Children select a napkin or ring and read the question to the group.

1. On which side of the plate does the napkin belong?

Answer: It goes to the left of the plate or under the fork.

2. When should the napkin be picked up and unfolded?

Answer: Wait for the host, the person who invited you or who is in charge, to pick up their napkin. Then you can.

3. What if the napkin is too big for my lap, what should I do?

Answer: Just fold it in half and place on your lap.

4. Do I use the napkin all folded up or do I shake it out?

Answer: Avoid shaking the napkin to open it. Just unfold it and slip it on your lap.

5. Should I take the napkin if the food is being served?

Answer: Yes, take the napkin off the table if the food is being served.

6. What do I do with the napkin when I have to leave the table?

Answer: Leave the napkin on the chair or on the table to the left of your plate. Also put it to the left of your plate when you're done eating, never on the plate.

7. It is OK to tuck the napkin in my collar?

Answer: Put the napkin on your lap. Tuck it into your shirt collar only if your host or hostess encourages it, usually because the food is very messy.

8. Is it ok to blow your nose in a cloth napkin?

Answer: Do not blow your nose into a cloth napkin.

9. What do I do with the napkin ring?

Answer: When you are done eating, it is polite to place your used napkin back in the ring.

10. Is there a special way to use a napkin?

Answer: It is not to be used like a washcloth. Wipe your mouth by dabbing.

Napkin folding

Give each child a napkin let them experiment folding.

5 Point Folded Napkin.

Fold square cloth napkin in half and in half again.

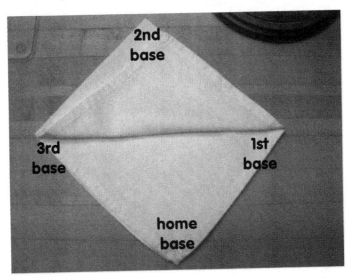

Using top layer fold up from home base to 2nd base.

Fold next layer up to almost 2nd base

Fold all layers up to 2nd base

Fold 1ˢᵗ base back behind napkin

Fold 3ʳᵈ base to the back of napkin. This napkin can lay flat or stand upright.

Open gifts *(allow 20 minutes)*

Have your camera ready.

After gift opening *(20 minutes)*

An active game or finishing projects will work well now.

End of party *(10 minutes)*

A fun activity such as watching a video of the party will bring the event to a close.

Be sure guests have goodie bags and everything they came with

Backward Party

Backward Party

Join the fun for Lisa's Birthday
Wear your clothes backwards, inside out
or reversed front to back.

Party ending at 2:00

Starting at 4:00

May 23

Please reply\RSVP
May 18th to 000-0000 or email

Sample Ave.

ABC Street

Start Street

Use mirror writing to create the invitation. You and your child can write them yourselves or use a computer program. Write the invitation, hold it against a window and trace the words, so it is backwards, copy and use as invitations.

Write on outside of envelope:
Mirror needed to read invitation!

Backward party

Nothing is more fun than this crazy mixed-up party. Discuss some ideas and come up with all kinds of backwards crazy things. This party can work well with 4th – 7th graders.

Plan for the day of the party

Welcome the guests with a big, "Glad you enjoyed the party wish you didn't have to leave" backward greeting!

Welcoming activity *(about 10 minutes)*

- For guests waiting for others to arrive. Have nametags available and ask the children to write their names backwards.

Set the theme *(optional 10-15 minutes)*

- Write down what you plan to do: watch a DVD backwards or read a story backwards.

Fun fact:

Special shoes were made for the US military during wartime with backward footprints on the sole. When being tracked, the troops looked like they were going the other way!

Activities and games *(allow 10 to 15 minutes per game plan on 30 to 45 minutes total)*

1. ***Make facemasks*** to be worn on the back of the head.

2. ***Make masks***, glue onto sunglasses, wear normally or on top of the head.

3. ***Make a list of palindrome words***, words that read backwards the same as forward: dad, mom, racecar, refer, deed, pop, etc.

4. ***Have a backwards race***: Walk backwards one way and return hopping backwards.

5. ***Draw backwards***: start a drawing a person from the shoes up.

6. ***Play musical chairs*** but instead of stopping when the music stops, they must walk backwards around chairs until the music starts.

   Materials needed: sunglasses, paper, yarn, markers, scissors, glue, paper, pencils, music and chairs.

Menu for meal or snack *(allow 20 minutes)*

* Be sure to start with singing "Happy Birthday" and eating dessert first. Follow the cake with sandwiches made with bread in the middle and wrapped with cheese and meat.

Open gifts *(allow 20 minutes)*

* Have your camera ready.

Activities *(15 – 30 minutes)*

* A game, or finish projects.

   1. ***A backwards game***: "How fast can you spell your name backwards." Use a stopwatch and have the children time one another. Try saying or have all sing the alphabet backwards. Awards go to the team that comes in last.

   2. ***Take photos of the children facing away from the camera.*** Ask the children write a thank you-note to the birthday child.

End of party (10 minutes)

Before parent pick up time. Be sure to welcome the children to the party and tell them how much fun they are going to have.

Observe that each child goes home with expected adult.

19

Games of Chance Party

Games of Chance

You are invited to
Jack's Birthday Party

July 24 • 4:00 pm

123 ABC Street
Fun Town, USA
(map is enclosed)

RSVP July 14
000-000-0000 or email

Chances are...
you will find the party
if you flow these
directions:

ABC Street
Town, USA

Print and glue the information on one
side of playing cards and send in an
envelope.

Games of Chance Party plan

Welcoming activity

- *Craft project:* Make a container for holding candy coins, markers, or small pads of paper and pencils to record scores. It can be as simple as manila envelope with a clasp. Have colored pens and such to embellish, and be sure to write the owner's name on the outside.

- Upon arrival, give your guests a supply of candy coins or small pads of paper and pencils.

- *Set the theme:* Games of chance are a great way to introduce probability, understanding the mathematical likelihood of an event occurring. A game of chance is any game where the result is influenced by a randomized device such as dice, a spinning top, playing cards, numbered balls falling from a container, etc. When a game of chance involves wagering money or valuables it becomes gambling. But keeping score or recording results is not gambling.

Games and activities

Explain the different games and the rules for each. Encourage everyone to try all the games of chance. Playing "21" increases quick addition skills; flipping coins teaches probability—the chances of getting heads is the same as the probability of getting tails; and rolling dice assists in learning about probability.

Older siblings or adults can assist in explaining game rules.

Set up areas for the different games available. Encourage the guests to move from place to place to try each.

- *Play "21"*

- *Dice game "Beat That"* Have a child roll three dice, trying to make the highest number possible. Example: roll 3-9-2 and rearrange dice to read 932. Pass dice to next child and say "Beat that." If they do, record each win by giving a marker to the winner. Pass to the right around the group. Then play for the smallest number.

- *Dice game "Special Me."* Each child rolls two dice, and the number they roll becomes their special number. If someone already has the number, roll again. Have the youngest roll first. A player who rolls somebody else's special number gives a chip to that person. Play the game for a few rounds so the children begin to recognize the probability of winning more than once.

- *Bingo*: Set up an area for playing.

- Create some activities to practice approximating. The more children practice the skill of estimating the better they become.

  - Fill a glass jar with gum balls-have guests write their estimate of how many on a slip of paper.

  - Use small individual packages of candy: have the children estimate how many candies are in their bag, open, count and eat!

  - Estimate how long a minutes is. Have the children raise their hand when they think a minute is up. Try 3 minutes.

  - Estimate how many stairs are in the stairway, how many doors are in your house, how many windows, etc

  - Estimate how long a friend can balance standing on one foot.

Meal or snack

Set up a buffet offering a number of easy to eat items that can be placed on a plate and do not require knives. This allows for easy snacks while keeping hands free for playing the different games.

Open gifts *(allow 20 minutes)*

Have your camera ready.

After gift opening

Continue playing games or award prizes to those with the most candy coins or highest or lowest scores at the end of the party. Award prizes for many categories—for the winners and the unlucky or unskilled!

End of party *(10 minutes before parent pick-up time)*

Observe that each child goes home with expected adult.

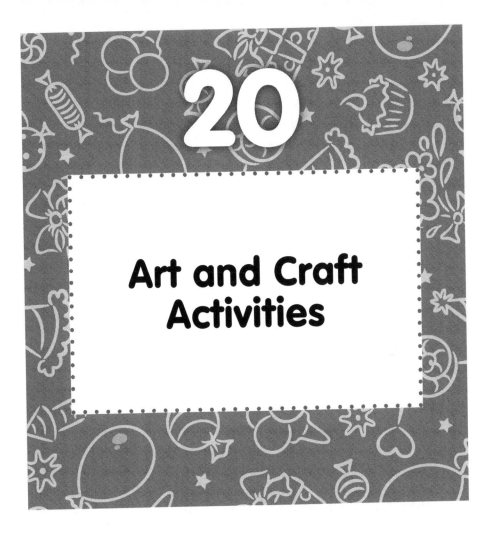

Bead making

Use scrapbook paper, colored paper, and magazine pages to create beautiful beads. You will need a darning needle, pencil, yarn, thread, and scissors.

Cut triangles out of decorative paper. Using an isosceles triangle the base of the triangle is the width of the bead; ¾ – 1 inch is a good size. Beginning with the base wrap the paper around a pencil or coffee stirrer. Wrap and put a drop of glue on the pointed end. Allow to dry. Another method uses a light layer of glue on the paper so the bead stays together while wrapping. Avoid putting glue on the area making contact with the pencil, straw or stirrer. The size of the item used to wrap the bead around defines the size of the finished interior hole.

Big feet

Create large feet for children to wear over their own shoes. Using tissue boxes the children can slip their feet through the preexisting slit on the top of the box. Cut off the bottom of the box so the child's feet make contact with the ground while wearing their big feet. Decorate in advance or have the children decorate. They will need to remove their shoes for a moment to slip their feet through the slat. Their shoe can be put on after slipping foot through the big feet.

Chalk drawing and graffiti drawing on the sidewalk

Give the children colored chalk and a space to create.

There is a freedom in drawing all over the sidewalk or driveway knowing it will be washed away with the next rain.

Cotton drawstring bag

These bags can be made in varied sizes and used for anything from a handbag to a jewelry bag. Select a printed fabric about 22 inches by 7 inches wide. Fold fabric right sides facing each other, pin and stitch sides together. Fold top of bag down 1 in tucking in raw edge to create casing. Pin and sew casing. To complete bag add 1 yard of ribbon or cord. Cut ribbon in half. Attach a safety pin into one end of the cord to assist threading. Thread one piece clockwise through both sides. Then start at other open end and thread second cord through both sides. Then tie ends and gently pull cords.

Decorate a brick

Use traditional bricks or cement blocks. Decorated brick can become a doorstop, bookends, or paperweight.

What you need: Bricks, fabric, felt, glue, paper, markers, yarn, etc.

Free-form plaster

Create your own three-dimensional sculpture animals. Mix plaster, stir until thick, and pour into a plastic bag and close it securely. Squish and squeeze the bag and make a shape for your animal. Open bag before it totally hardens and poke in pipe cleaners or Popsicle sticks for legs. Remove from bag when hard and dry, then paint.

Hats

Paper party hat is made in advance of the party. Create a hat for each child using grocery bags or colored construction paper. To make a hat form use a mixing bowl approximately the size of your child's head. Prepare the construction paper or bag by dampening it with warm water. Mold the bag or paper over the mixing bowl, secure the paper until dry using a rubber band. Allow to dry overnight, longer if it's humid. Trim the edges of the dried hats to form brims.

Have the children decorate with silk flowers, ribbons, lace, tulle, fabric scraps, and or sequins. Tie ribbon around the brim and finish with a bow. Use white glue or with adult supervision use a glue gun.

• ***Marble painting.*** Select cardboard boxes large enough for the size paper you choose. Place paper, dishes of colored paints, and marbles nearby. Write child's name on the back of the paper. Have child select a marble, place marble in a dish with paint. Use a spoon to coat the marble with paint, lift marble out of paint, then place on paper in box lid. Roll marble around to make a design. Remove marble, rinse in soapy water and place in another color. Repeat process until happy with marble painting

Have a place ready for their artwork to dry.

Masks

Make masks, glue onto sunglasses, wear normally or on top of the head.

Napkin rings

Create useful napkin rings using the cardboard cylinder from aluminum foil roll. Cut the roll into 1½ inch pieces. Cut fabric in 3 inch widths. Glue fabric around the cylinder and tuck excess fabric inside.

Paper doll chain

Use a long strip of paper and fold accordion style — back and forth. Draw a person, making sure some of the drawing touches the fold. Cut design but don't cut anything on the fold.

Place cards

Use fancy paper or paper doilies, scissors, markers, glitter, glue and create a place card for each person at the table.

Play dough

Combine 1 cup flour, 1 cup water, 1 tablespoon oil, 2 teaspoons cream of tartar, ½ cup salt, and food coloring or liquid tempera paint to desired color.

Add color to water in sauce pan. Add in all other ingredients, and cook over medium heat. Stir constantly until mixture forms into a ball on the stirring spoon. Remove from heat and place on wax paper. Cool. Knead until smooth. Store in airtight plastic bag or container. No refrigeration needed. For extra fun add glitter or flavored extract to the water. Cooking time approximately 3-5 minutes.

Puppets

Make out of paper bags, socks, mittens, a finger from a glove, etc.

Added materials: scissors, scraps of felt, fabric, scrapbook papers, buttons, pipe cleaners, yarn, Popsicle sticks, wire, markers, Styrofoam ball, etc.

Puppet stage

- Create a stage by draping an old sheet over a table. Cut out a rectangle for the stage area. Children sit under table to perform with their puppet. Have the children take turns being on stage.

- Get a big box, large enough for children to fit in, and cut a hole for the stage.

Sand casting

Create a design, make a mold of your foot or hand, your own fossils, use sea shells, etc.

What you will need: sand, plaster, water, a container to hold the sand.

Fill the container with moist sand. Make a hand print by pressing your hand about an inch into wet sand. Mix the plaster until it is thick, then pour it into the depression. Wait about 45 minutes and carefully pick it out of the sand and dust it off.

Surprise balls

Colorful balls made of crepe paper strips wrapped in layers around small gifts. When unwrapped the toys are revealed as the layers are removed. Start with: a plastic egg filled with a toy, a small ball or a yoyo. Wrap using crepe paper strips around the center item securing the first strip with tape. After a few layers insert a balloon, small toy, fake mustache, small charm, gum, candy, or sticker to the next layer, wrapping until all toys in their containers are wrapped inside the surprise ball. The ball may become lumpy. The balls will all have the same items, but will not be in the same order so, when exchanged, each child will have the surprise of discovery. The fun of this activity is in assembling the balls and interacting with one another while doing it.

Tie-dyeing

Tie-dyeing T-shirts or socks:

Use white cotton fabric for best results. Secure tightly pleated, folded or squished fabric with rubber bands. The fabric covered by the rubber bands resist the dye. Dip or submerge fabric into dye bath, using rubber gloves. Add more rubber bands and dip into another color. Using two colors helps to prevent a muddy look. Allow to dry. Have plastic bags available for taking any damp cloth home.

Dyeing fabric for younger children: Use white fabric or tissue paper. Fold the paper lengthwise and along the width as many times as possible. Mix fabric dye in small containers, and dip corners of the folded fabric into different colors. Unfold the fabric and dry on newspaper.

Use finished fabric for decorating a brick, personal journal, frame, or just to enjoy.

Weave a placemat

Fancy ribbons can be used for the placemat. Select two sheets of construction paper. Fold one in half (the folded section will be more of a square than a rectangle) keeping it folded start at the fold edge cut leaving about an inch on either side and at the end uncut. Repeat cutting one inch apart, minding not to cut all the way to the end, just an inch short of the edge. Using the second piece of construction paper cut into 1 inch strips to be used to weave. Start weaving the strips of 1 inch paper, move the strips over and under, then over and under again. Start the next strip going under and then over, then under and over until complete. Use a bit of ribbon to add to the exquisiteness of the mat. A dot of glue on each end will keep it together.

Game Ideas

All games may be modified to fit the group. Games of elimination leave a number of children with nothing to do, and young children may wander off. To avoid this situation have a new child become "it" every time someone is found, caught, or tagged. Young children do not expect prizes for games, they will enjoy the fun of playing the games. Tell assisting adults if you are modifying the rules of a game.

Bean bag relay

Children enjoy movement. Games of movement that use up energy can be played inside using everyday items. Create a relay game using a bean bag chair or an overstuffed pillow. Have the children line up, then one at a time race to the chair, sit down, and race back to the start. The children will enjoy watching each other flop into the big chair and then race back to the group. No winner, no looser, just a lot of giggles and fun.

Dozing dogs

All the children, except for two who will be dog trackers, lie on the floor in sleeping positions. Once comfortably settled, they are not to move. The dog trackers walk through the room and try to make the sleeping dogs laugh and thereby move, telling them jokes and so on. The dog trackers are not allowed to touch the dogs. Dogs caught moving get up and join the trackers.

Follow the leader

The children line up behind the leader and while moving around the room or rooms must follow all the leader's actions.

Example:

- Walk around winding the line like a snake or S shape.

- Clap your hands above your head, then wave your arms at your side.

- Hop on one foot and tap your head as you spiral around the room.

- Tap your feet, stomp your feet, shake a leg, and keep looking back to be sure the kids are attempting to follow you. Ask a child to be a leader.

Go fish

Create a fishing pole using a stick or pole, tie a string to one end, and attach a magnet to the string. Make fish using paper and attach paper clips to each. Have the children go fishing.

Hide and seek

One child is selected to be it, the person who will do the seeking. He or she turns around a few times, hands covering eyes, and counts to 25 while standing at the established base, while everyone hides. Then, saying "Ready or not, here I come." the seeker starts looking. When children are found, the children can assist in finding others. The first child found becomes the new it.

Hokey-Pokey

For young children the instructions to "make a circle" may need additional guidance. Have the children line up then ask them to clasp hands. While holding the hand of the first child walk over to the child at the end of the line. An instant circle! The hokey-Pokey is a song combined with movement.

With everyone in the circle sing, "Put your right hand in (the circle), put your right hand out, put your right hand in and shake it all about. Do the hokey pokey (put hands above your head and shake them with hands open and fingers wiggling) and turn yourself about, that's what it's all about."

Left hand, right foot, left foot, backside in, front side in, head, elbows, etc.

For young children who don't know right from left: "put your hand in, put your hand out, put your hand in and shake it all about. Put the other hand in, etc."

Hop Scotch

Object of the game is to move your marker up to the 10 on the Hop Scotch board. Using sidewalk chalk, draw a game board on a drive way, patio, or garage floor. How to draw the game board. The size of each square is about 12 inches. Put a 1 in the bottom square, squares 2 and 3 are next to each other horizontally centered above the 1 square, square 4 centered above the 2 and 3, then squares 5 and 6 next to each other centered and above square 4. Next, square 7 centered above the squares 5 and 6. Squares 8 and 9 are next to each other centered above square 7. Last is square 10 on the top. How to Play: Player uses a special rock or bean bag for their marker. First player throws his rock onto the 1, then jumps over square one, then lands on 2 and 3 with each foot in a square, then one foot on the 4, then with each foot in a square land on 5 and 6, then hop with one foot on 7, then with each foot in a square jump onto 8 and 9, then with both feet on 10, then turn around. Move down the hopscotch board until you get to the 2 and 3 bend over and pick up your marker and jump off the board with your marker in your hand. The next person takes a turn. Proceed taking turns moving marker onto the next number, jumping over the square the maker is on. If marker doesn't land on correct square or child cannot balance while picking up marker, they lose a turn. The next person goes, next turn, begin on the number missed on the last turn.

Hunting games

Plan to hide at least 6 items per child. In advance of the party hide the items in a specific area. When it is time for the hunt give each child a container to hold the items they find. Show the children an example of what they will be looking for and what rooms or areas they can hunt in. To avoid a child finding too many or too few hidden treasures let them know there is a limit. When they have found their limit they can assist the rest of the children. The first to find 6 can win a prize or get a big round of applause from the group.

I Spy hunt game: Give the guests a list of items to find in a specific area planned for the hunt. Explain they are to observe the items without removing or moving them. Older guests can write down what room they found the item. Hand out compasses and record the cardinal points and ordinal points where items were found.

Musical chairs

The traditional musical chairs game is set up using one less chair than children playing. The chairs are placed back to back in a row with the seats facing opposite directions.

Use sturdy chairs to ensure safety.

Rules: The children are to walk around the chairs while music is playing. When the music stops they sit down. Play until just one child remains.

Variation for young children: The premise of an elimination game is to have a winner; this creates the need for prizes as well as a lot of idle time for the children eliminated. Try this non elimination version.

Start with a practice round with as many chairs as children so everyone meets with success. Then remove one chair. To keep the eliminated child enthused have them assist you with turning the music on and off. Do not remove additional chairs. Instead have the newly eliminated child switch places with another child. Young children will enjoy the activity of finding an empty chair. Play the game for about 10-15 minutes.

Pin the tail on the donkey

Create a poster sized donkey to hang on the wall, be sure to omit the tail. Give each child a tail with double sided tape on the back and their name on the front. One child at a time is blindfolded and tries to attach the tail on the donkey as close to the spot where it belongs. The tail closest is the winner. This game works best with small groups, waiting for each child to be blindfolded and contemplating where to place their tail can take a long time.

Red light, green light

Children line up on a line approximately 40 feet away from the child giving the commands, who is "it." The goal of the game is to swiftly move toward "it" when given the green light and be the first to tag "it." The child who is "it" stands with their back to the others, and shouts "Green light," whereupon the children move forward until the red light command is given. "It" says "Red light" while quickly turning toward the group, and if any children are observed moving they are sent back to the start line.

Relay races

Two teams play against each other in competitive racing activities. There needs to be a defined starting line, a turnaround spot and at least two people per team. The children choose teams, line up one after the other behind the starting line. When told to "go" one child from each team performs the task of the relay traveling to the turnaround spot returning to the start tagging the next person in line to perform the task attempting to return to the starting line before the members of the other team. Playground cones work well to identify boundary lines.

Remember items on the tray game

Place a number of items on a tray. Have the children look at them. Tell them you are going to remove the tray and they can try to remember what was on the tray. Remove or cover the tray with a cloth. Give the children paper and pencils. Have then write or draw as many items as they remember. See who did the best, work in teams, give a prize to the highest number remembered. For young children cover the tray and have them take turns sharing what they remember seeing.

Tag

A designated area for this running game needs to be established, such as the tree on this side, the chair over here, the fence, and the wall. One child is selected to be "it." The other children run while "it" tries to tag someone. If tagged that child becomes the new"it". Continue game and end before they loose interest.

Simon says

Play with 3 or more children. One person becomes Simon and gives directions to the other children. Each statement that should be followed must be prefaced with the words "Simon says" (jump on one foot, clap hands, jump up and down, tap your head) Simon quickly gives commands Simon says clap your hands, the children follow, then Simon just gives a command without saying Simon Says, the children who respond are eliminated. Children are eliminated by not responding when hearing "Simon says" or they respond when the words "Simon says" were not used. The last child still in the game becomes Simon.

Trees and squirrels

Divide the children into 2/3 trees and 1/3 squirrels. Choose someone to be the person to say "Go." Have sets of children hold hands to become a tree, when told to "Go" the squirrels need to find an empty tree, one squirrel to a tree. The child (squirrel) left with no tree becomes the person to say "Go" Remember there are always less trees than squirrels when playing this game.

After a few rounds, switch one tree person into a squirrel and have the squirrels become part of the trees.

Supply/Shopping List

Items to consider having on hand
Highlight items you may need

Basic party goods:

- Tablecloths
- Plates
- Cups
- Napkins
- Utensils
- Invitations
- Plastic resealable bags
- Party hats
- Envelopes
- Stamps
- Food
- Balloons
- Banner decorations
- Streamers
- Party favors
- Extra scissors
- Project materials
- Boxes, bins
- Goodie bags
- Camera

Basic supplies for art and crafts:

- Crayons
- Tempera paint
- Clay dough
- Art aprons
- Brushes
- Cups for paint
- Paper
- Markers
- Tissue paper
- Construction paper

- Glitter
- Stamps
- Stamp pads
- Masking tape
- Drop cloth
- White glue
- Washable paint
- Scissors
- Colored pencils
- Sticks
- Sponges

- Beads
- Craft sticks
- Yarn
- Felt
- Chalk
- Foam brushes
- Stickers
- Pipe cleaners
- Elastic cord
- Oat cereal & macaroni

Basic supplies for active play:

- Balls
- Jump ropes
- Bean bags
- Foam balls
- Sidewalk chalk
- Frisbees
- Music
- Rackets

- Blocks
- Yo-yo
- Paddle
- Ball
- Bubbles
- Hula hoop
- Jacks
- Kites

- Jigsaw puzzles
- Bean bag
- Poster board
- Clothespins
- Bottle
- Scarves
- Cloths
- Play area cones

23

Invitation Templates

These templates may be used for invitations and thank you notes. Remove template, add text, make needed copies, and have your child or family decorate each invitation. For several invitations it may be easier for a child to decorate one invitation and make multiple copies. Scan the template to increase the size, to add a photo of your child, to color and add text. Be creative and have fun!

Color templates are available on our website at LibbyandPenny.com. Continue visiting our website for new templates and party ideas.

You are invited

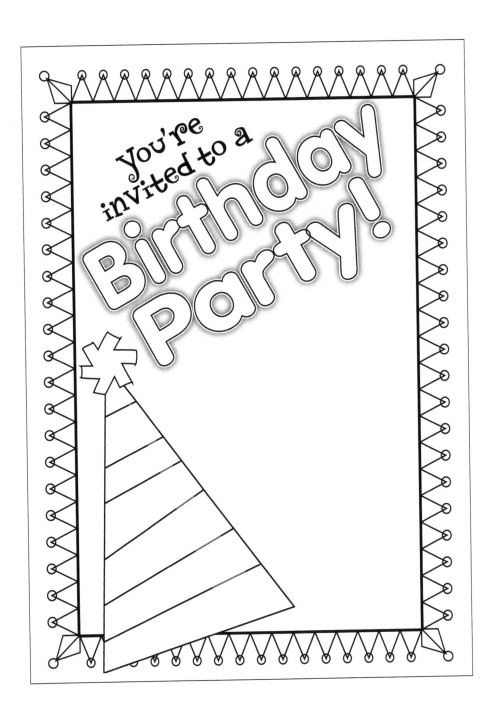

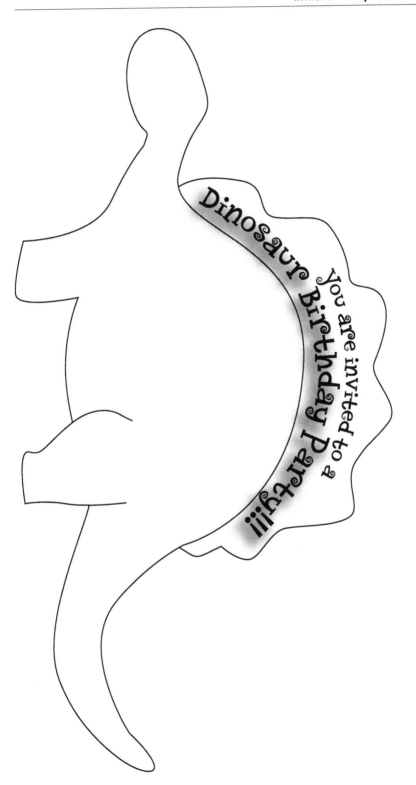

Be an Artist Party

We will be painting, so please wear appropriate clothes.

Fancy Dress-Up Tea Party

Dress in fancy dress-up party clothes

Hats, gloves and shiny shoes will all be welcome.

Recipe for a Great Birthday Party

NOTES:

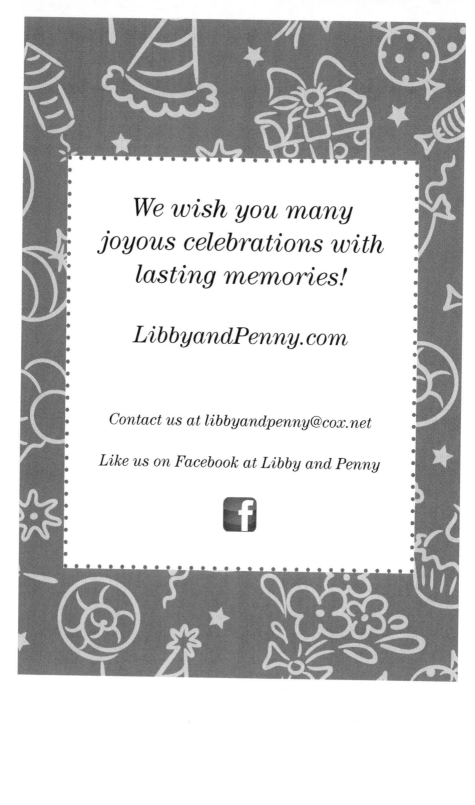

We wish you many joyous celebrations with lasting memories!

LibbyandPenny.com

Contact us at libbyandpenny@cox.net

Like us on Facebook at Libby and Penny

34166627R00096

Made in the USA
Middletown, DE
10 August 2016